Precious Are God's Plans

by
Lea Fowler

QUALITY PUBLICATIONS
P.O. BOX 1060
ABILENE, TEXAS 79604
(915) 677-6262

ISBN: 0-89137-440-X

FOREWORD

Due to current pressures of "women's rights," we often conform to the teachings of the day, not realizing the final outcome of our choices.

May our Father help us to understand that "His rights" will give us "exceeding abundantly beyond all that we ask or think according to the power that works within us" Ephesians 3:20.

DEDICATED TO:

The Holy Planner and Architect of our lives.

GRATITUDE

To my daughter, Becky, who labored in typing, grammar, and punctuation.

To the rest of the family, Russ, Tom, and Judy who kept nudging and encouraging me.

To Martha, my first mentor, and Fran, my last one.

To Liz, my lovely listener to both books.

To Nita M. – the worthiest of women.

To the many women who have written or encouraged me to write these things down.

TABLE OF CONTENTS

INTRODUCTION

God has great plans for His daughters. How it must hurt Him to see us cut off our blessings because of lack of knowledge or desire for patience.

"For I know the plans that I have for you," declares the Lord, "plans for welfare and not for calamity to give you a future and a hope."

"Then you will call upon me and come and pray to me, and I will listen to you."

"And you will seek me and find me, when you search for me with all your heart. And I will be found by you," declares the Lord.

— Jeremiah 29:11-14

All biblical quotations are taken from the New American Standard Version unless otherwise noted.

MY PLANS FOR YOU

I knew you when you first loved me
And sought to do my will.
Your hand took mine as we traveled
Together up the hill.
The climb has not always been pleasant;
There's been storms and thunder and rain
And times when you thought the trip futile
Because of the trials and pain.
But the longer we trudged up the mountain
And occasionally caught sight of the view,
The more you ceased to wonder
At the plans I still have for you.

— Lea Fowler

Chapter 1
BID THE OLDER WOMEN TO TEACH THE YOUNGER WOMEN

Titus, you encourage the older women, who have God's qualifications for teaching, to teach the younger Christian women what is lacking in their young lives.

Older women likewise are to be reverent in their behavior, not malicious gossips, nor enslaved to much wine, teaching what is good, that they may encourage the young women to love their husbands, to love their children, to be sensible, pure, workers at home, kind, being subject to their own husbands, that the word of God may not be dishonored.

— *Titus 2:3-5*

God, who knows all, knows that love is a decision, a learned art. We *learn* to love our husbands, our children, and our homes — maybe. We love ourselves by instinct, by nature.

If love is learned, who will teach us? If we had a loving mother, we have been blessed. Most people quickly identify true love with motherhood. Mothers sacrifice, deny themselves, and look for our good before their own.

However, God knows that a godly woman is one of the best teachers for young Christian women. Many young women have had no godly examples in their upbringing. They come in from the world, from the highways, and the hedges. They are eager to learn, yes, but know little about real love.

REVERENT IN THEIR BEHAVIOR

Why should older women be reverent in *their behavior?* Because a silly woman is a natural part of youth. "Foolishness is not only bound in the heart of a child" — a short child, but also in many taller children — brides.

1

Many young ladies marry unable to cook, clean a house, please a husband or God. (When my youngest daughter went off to a Christian college, she was amazed at the mothers who came down every weekend to wash and iron their daughters' clothes!) They still giggle, sleep late, dream of the same things they dreamed of while they were single – pretty clothes, good times and the opposite sex. Soap operas know that these subjects entice the immature, and they deal hearty portions of the three daily: pretty clothes, good times, and sex. Take these things out of soap operas, and there would be no soap!

But when we become a woman – an older Christian woman, especially, we must put away childish things.

I remember a class of teenage girls that I taught years ago. Several were seniors in high school, and some of their classmates were getting married in the near future. The girls were twittering excitedly about marriage and the advantages of being "freed brides" instead of "chained children." I asked them to close their eyes and then said something like this:

"How many of you are ready to leave home? Ready for the bridal shower, the wedding, your first apartment, a young man who adores you, and freedom from parental discipline? Ready to leave home and make your own decisions?"

Almost every girl eagerly raised her hand.

"Close your eyes once more. Now, let your mind go to your mother. How many are ready to swap places with her? Ready to do her work and bear all of her responsibilities? Look at her closet – ready to exchange wardrobes with her? Are you willing to be in subjection to an older man like your father? Are you ready to settle for her entertainments and lack of them and ready to make her sacrifices?"

Not a hand was raised – only sober faces looked at me. (I wonder how these girls are doing now as they follow mother's footsteps!)

NOT MALICIOUS GOSSIPS

"I know we are not supposed to repeat anything unless it is good, but THIS IS GOOD!" Gossip is so delicious, so interesting, so shocking, so much fun when we are young, and if we are not careful, when we're older. God said older women have to work on this, and He knows us.

But older women, older godly women, should know the danger of gossip and the repercussions that can develop. The end result can be destroyed lives, a family break-up, suicide, divorce, or a lost soul. (The lost soul could be the gossiper's!)

God tells us that a good name is better than riches. Shakespeare says that when you steal a man's purse, you steal trash – but when you steal his good name, you do him irreparable damage. (Somehow, the Chinese know how to teach their children to live in such a way that they will never dishonor the family name. I wish we could learn that!)

Malicious gossip is the worst of all! It hopes to hurt; it does not care what the consequences may be. It enjoys another's misfortune – and willfully repeats and embellishes the current story. It does not hesitate to "murder" the reputation of another, even of another child of God's.

How can we expect the young women to want to confide in a gossipy old woman who will tell it all? How can they expect help from the tale bearer? "The words of a whisperer are like dainty morsels, and they go down into the innermost parts of the body" (Proverbs 18:8).

Older women who are going to be helpful to God must remember how hard it is to be young. They must remember that all of us still sin daily and fall short of the glory of God. They must remember how awful it is to not know the answers that are so easily understood in later life because of practice and lessons learned through trial and error. You can never be an effective counselor if you are easily shocked or cannot remember the sins of your own youth.

"Rejoice, young man, during your childhood, and let your heart be pleasant during the days of young manhood. And follow the impulses of your heart and the desires of your eyes. Yet know that God will bring you to judgment for all these things. So, remove vexation from your heart and put away pain from your body, because childhood and the prime of life is fleeting" (Ecclesiastes 11:9,10). Of course, this applies to young women, too.

Good women must be able to see the end of a distressing situation and to know that WHATEVER it is – it could happen to you or yours! How can *we* expect mercy if we have not been merciful? I have known older Christian women who kept the wedding dates on the calendar to be sure the first baby wasn't born too soon. And I have also seen these same women have this come back into their own families.

Mothers and grandmothers make such a mistake when they assure everyone that their offspring would never do such and such. They underestimate the power of Satan and overestimate the strength of their children. Only God knows the scope of the sins *we* have yet to commit.

Families tend to spread their wings over their own while they are in trouble because "love does cover a multitude of sins." The older woman should realize that her love must cover the sins of others, too – especially the sins of the family of God. She should sympathize with the tears and heartbreak of the situation and forget the excitement of the gossip. She must remember – "there but by the grace of God go I" – or my children.

God tells us to weep with those who weep and rejoice with those who rejoice. A scripture that has always helped me at times of family sins, or

3

embarrassments or humiliations is found in Ecclesiastes 11:1,2. "Cast your bread on the surface of the waters for you will find it after many days. Divide your portion to seven, or even to eight, for you do not know what misfortune may occur on the earth."

This scripture is telling us that we had better share what we have with others (and that sharing can be kindness and mercy) because we don't know what is ahead of us. Share your love and understanding with seven or eight, and then when you need a friend, someone will reach for you with the same sort of love and understanding that you have shown to others.

RECIPROCATION

I met a stranger in the night
Whose lamp had ceased to shine.
I paused and let him light his lamp from mine.
A tempest sprung up later on
And shook the world about
And when the wind was gone — my lamp was out!
But back to me the stranger came.
His lamp was glowing fine!
He held the precious flame — and lighted mine.

— Anonymous

NOR ENSLAVED TO WINE

This portion of scripture puzzled me for years. How could any older godly woman who wanted to teach younger women be an alchoholic?

God is a realist. He knows what is going on in His world and in his family, the church. There have always been secret drinkers, and there always will be. Women, because of the double standard, especially want these addictions hidden.

Again, we must find mercy in our hearts for temptations that we don't have. No one can sympathize with another to the extent that is needed until he has had the same temptation. This is why the various support groups for drinking, gambling, overeating, etc. are so successful. A group is saying, "I know how bad it is because it had or has me hooked."

We, who may be smug about our self-control, may have to give second thoughts about our addictions to Valium or other doctor given prescriptions. Somehow, we are going to have to become "unaddicted." I remember a good woman coming to us for counsel who had been placed on drugs by her psychiatrist. We felt so sorry for her in her innocent predicament. It took a tremendous struggle for her to be freed again, but she made it —

4

and if I remember right, she did it "cold turkey."

Parents are warned by those who know that they are setting a bad example to their children if they are constantly popping pills – though it be only aspirin. Children are registering that pain must be overcome immediately.

Women of Bible times had a ready supply of wine at their fingertips. Wine was a way out from the present pain – whatever that pain was. It could have been the loss of a husband's love, the empty nest, boredom, depression, or just sheer loneliness. They didn't have television, a ready supply of reading matter, or telephones.

"Don't do it," God says. "You will cancel out your effectiveness. This is the time that you have to be among the greatest workers in the kingdom. Your husbands are still busy making the living, but you have almost unlimited time to be about your Father's business." As the old song goes – "Let your eyes see the need of workers today."

In 1 Timothy 2:10 it said, "But rather by good works as befits women making a claim to godliness." Older women, who are making such a claim, you are needed so badly. WHERE ARE YOU?

There are things that you can say to young Christian women that only YOU can say effectively. You are a living proof, a testimony, that the young can take to heart. You survived! You are happy, wise – well, wiser than you used to be; you've raised good children who are faithful or were when they lived with you; your husband loves you; your children love you; you've survived your heartbreaks; and yet you come to teach with a smile on your face. Come in.

"Help me to be a survivor, too, and to reap the same sort of blessings that God has poured out on you. I want peace and joy and kindness and security and my husband's love and my children's obedience and answers – today!" This is what the younger women are saying.

Maybe the reason they want you to say these things to them is because most women never outgrow their need for a Mama. I haven't, and I am sixty-six. (They say that a woman who will tell her age will tell anything.)

Probably, it is easier to hear an older woman teach submission than to hear the young preacher teach the same lesson!

Titus, teach the older woman what she lacks and then encourage her to go to the young women who want her and need her. They are tied in the house with noise and young children and earaches and bed-wetting! God knows what is needed, and He spells it out for the good of all.

WHERE ARE THE OLDER WOMEN?

In each generation the body of Christ should be restoring more fully the New Testament church. We must ever be in the process of following the given pattern of perfection laid out in the Scriptures.

Maybe one of the reasons we have not encouraged the older women to teach is because of the restrictions God has placed on women to not take the pulpit. The desire to please God is felt by the church, and so a restriction can cause us to go too far the other way and fail to fulfill the job given to women. It is easy to over-emphasize the "do nots" and leave undone the "do's."

There is a place for women to learn and to learn quietly. It has always been a principle of God's both in the Old and the New Testament that the men teach the assemblies. But, this should not nullify the teaching of God for older women to teach the younger women. There are as many women to be taught as men — if not more. The older woman has a mind-boggling assignment. She is to be busy helping to instruct the younger Christian women as well as discipling her world.

I've heard young Christian women say, "I don't want the older women teaching me." And I have heard older women say, "I don't want to teach the younger women. I've done my time." However, I haven't heard God say, "How would you ladies like for it to be done?"

> *Christian growth is not the struggle to become the kind of person we think God wants us to be, but a surrender of our bodies, all our faculties, our right to ourselves, to God that He may make us and mold us into the image of His son, that through us His life and love and grace might flow.*
>
> *— Rick Halvarson*

If we have the Spirit dwelling in us, then we should want to please our Father and should have the faith to know that His way works. It is in dying to self that we can become the workers that God desires us to be. Jesus set the perfect example to us all in obedience when He said, "Not my will, but Thine be done."

It is immaturity and lack of faith that makes us petulantly say, "But I don't want it that way."

"It is in our faults and failings, not in our virtues, that we touch one another and find sympathy" — Anonymous.

It used to be that all of the ladies' classes were taught by the preacher. I loved my men teachers and appreciated all the words of God that they shared with me. I was blessed with wonderful men teachers!

But, I'll never forget the first older, godly woman I heard teach. That sweet lady was Mrs. W. R. Smith, and she spoke at the ACU lectures in Abilene, Texas. It was probably about thirty-six years ago. I sat spellbound with tears streaming down my face. She taught four lessons on four different days. On the last day after the final lesson, I went to her and said, "If I lived next door to you, I know I would get to heaven." SHE TOUCHED MY SOUL!

> *The glory of life is brightest*
> *When the glories of life are dim,*
> *And she has most compelled me*
> *Who most has pointed to Him.*
>
> *She has held me, stirred me, swayed me,*
> *I have hung on her every word.*
> *'Til I fain would rise and follow not her,*
> *Not her, but her Lord.*
>
> *Anonymous*

And that's the way I felt. How much I would have been robbed if I had not heard godly *women* teach me publicly and privately!

We spend hundreds of dollars yearly to have preachers hold special meetings for the church. It is hoped that they, too, will touch our souls and renew our minds and activate our service for the Lord. They do well!

But why can't we be just as concerned to have our women taught by women? Women have more time, in time, to work for the Lord. A church with dedicated women will send out waves of good throughout the whole body of Christ. Husbands will be more loved, submitted to, and appreciated. Children will be more loved and more loveable, more obedient, more like Timothy when they are grown. Homes will be happier, lovelier, more hospitable, cleaner, more peaceful, and more anxious to be returned to. Women will mature faster, and the fruits of the Spirit will be more noticeable in their lives. God will be more glorified in His daughters.

Why don't we encourage such wonders? It could be for several reasons or combination of reasons. We may not *know* what Titus teaches; we may not believe it; or we may fear that women should be content with things as they are lest harm come from increased activities. There is probably, no doubt, that there would be somewhere, sometime, mistakes made, but the good would far outweigh the bad. And, we would be pleasing God by our obedience to His word. *God's way works, and faith believes it.* (It is true that there would have to be a new item included in the budget, but the benefits would warrant it. God's money should be used to carry out God's teachings.)

There may be a few women who feel they are "called to preach." (I don't know of one personally.) Most women have great difficulty to just stand before an audience of women, let alone having the desire to speak to the whole church. Most of us, especially when we are older, realize our limitations: our speaking voices, our emotions which are easily triggered, our lack of physical strength, and just the recognition that it is not fitting that we place ourselves where God did not place us. (If I had my "ruthers," I would never speak from the pulpit but would speak on floor level to the women. However, many times this is not possible because of the P.A. systems. I'm just more comfortable on the lower level.)

We need to remember that God does not specify whether the teaching should be public or private. Many good women could never speak to any group but could and would drop in and reason with a troubled young woman. It is advantageous to have a large group of ladies taught at one time, but the smaller teaching situations are very necessary, too.

Much that the older woman will have to say will be words of experience. Day to day living is a great teacher. Even our past mistakes can work together for the good of others. We are learning every day in positive and negative ways. We have obeyed God and reaped the benefits, and we have occasionally listened to Satan and reaped his woes.

Some young Christian women have godly mothers who have instructed them and do instruct them, but many of us are first generation Christians. We have had to learn it the hard way.

It is time now – past time – that the hard way be put away, and God's way of short cuts be followed. It is an old saying – "The things we learned by experience we probably should not have had to learn in the first place." Too true.

There is a terrific program now among many of the southern congregations called Lads to Leaders and Lassies to Leaderettes, organized by Jack Zorn of Montgomery, Alabama. It is designed to train our youth to be effective public speakers. They learn to get over stage fright and to think on their feet. I have seen some of these young people in action – both boys and girls – and was very impressed with them! How many of us would have benefitted from such a program when we were young!

Some ladies won't hear, and you can't "learn" anybody. Some will never want to learn. They would rather do it their way and suffer. So be it. But for those who want to learn and better themselves and be spared bitter reaping and be happier in the learning – then come and let us study together and reason together about a better way.

Let us turn to the list of subjects and qualities that young women need to be aware of so that they can consciously see their needs. God fashioned women with His own hands, and it increases our faith to read *His list* of what we need to work on. The Creator *knows* and *loves* and *understands* the created. May we trust our souls and bodies to His care and instructions.

We will never try to amend what we do not know is amiss.

8

THOUGHT QUESTIONS

1. Have you ever had an older, godly woman help you?

2. Would you rather be helped privately or publicly by an older woman?

3. Are *you* aspiring to be a godly woman?

Chapter 2
TO LOVE THE WORTHY WOMAN

The last chapter of Proverbs introduces us to God's ideal of womankind. When we first meet her, she humbles us terribly. We do not desire to emulate her, for she seems to be the "impossible dream." In our immaturity some might even ridicule her, or try to bring her down. Maturity loves her, appreciates her, and gradually even imitates her. She leads the way to complete fulfillment and happiness for her family, community, and for herself. In time she becomes our friend.

WHO WROTE IT?

Proverbs 31:1 says that these are the words of King Lemuel and that these words were an oracle, taught to him by his mother. Interestingly enough, this could have been told to Solomon by Bathsheba. Lemuel means "God is bright," and this could be a symbolic name for Solomon.

According to (Bible commentator) Matthew Henry, she spoke like this: "Thou are descended from me, thou art the son of my womb, and therefore what I say comes from the authority and affection of a parent. Thou art a piece of myself. Be wise and good and then I am well paid. Thou art the son of my vows – the son I prayed God to give me and promised to give back to God."

Good women, *most* women, want their sons to marry well. They want them to have a happy home, a loving wife, a well kept house, and obedient children who are a credit to the family name. God wants that, too, for *His* sons who wear His name.

As we carefully study these important lessons, note that the bride's beauty is not mentioned as an asset to be desired. Rather, at the end of the discourse it is said, "Charm is deceitful and beauty is vain, but a woman who fears the Lord, she shall be praised" (Proverbs 31:30).

11

In the musical "Fiddler on the Roof," a story of Jewish living, the young girl wanted the matchmaker to find her a handsome man, but the mother wanted him to be a scholar. That is the way with all youth – "Will they be handsome or beautiful," and the cautious parent says – "Will they be much more than that?"

Someone has well written, "To be a mother of men, a woman must make men of her boys. She demands their best, not because it belongs to her, but because it is due them. For that which is due children is not ease and luxury but hardening of muscles, the habit of work, a sense of honor and a self-respect born of integrity" – Anonymous.

If these words were written to Solomon, it does not appear that he took his mother's counsel. With all the wives and concubines that he had, he made the statement,

> And I discovered more bitter than death the woman whose heart is snares and nets, whose hands are chains. One who is pleasing to God will escape from her, but the sinner will be captured by her. 'Behold, I have discovered this,' says the Preacher, 'adding one thing to another to find an explanation, which I am still seeking but have not found. I have found one man among a thousand, but I have not found a woman among all these. Behold, I have found only this, that God made men upright, but they have sought out many devices.
>
> – Ecclesiastes 7:26-29

Careful study reveals he is speaking of an adulterous woman, the strange woman, but I can't help but wonder if Solomon looked in the right places for a wife. Did he ever seek the little Jewish virgin who was raised right and would have made him the worthy wife? It must have been an almost impossible thing for him to seek an average wife when he had access to the beauties of the universe. He could have had "Miss Israel," "Miss Egypt," and "Miss Universe."

WHO CAN FIND AN EXCELLENT WIFE?

"An excellent wife, who can find? For her worth is far above jewels" (Proverbs 31:10). The King James Version puts it a virtuous wife. The word virtuous means a woman of strength. Matthew Henry says of that verse, "A virtuous woman is a woman of spirit, who has the command of her own spirit and knows how to manage other's. A virtuous woman is a woman of resolution, who, having espoused good principles, is firm and steady to them. Who can find her?"

My question is – how many young men would seek her or pursue her if they found her? Here is a woman of strength. (Young men like to feel their

12

mothers are virtuous, strong, and uncompromising, but they seldom seek a sweetheart of the same cloth.) It would take a man of strength to seek a woman of strength.

Mr. Henry continues, "Good women are scarce. But he that designs to marry ought to take heed that he be not biased by beauty or gaiety, wealth or parentage, dressing well or dancing well; for all these may be and yet the woman not be virtuous. The more rare good wives are the more they are to be valued."

(Matthew Henry's comments fascinate me. He wrote in the 1600's, and died at the age of fifty-two. However, comments on the Scriptures are never out of date for the Word does not change or lose its meaning.)

There is no way that we will ever restore to society the arranging of our children's marriages. But with the divorce rate being one out of two marriages, and the threat of it becoming even greater, what can we do to see that our daughters are virtuous and our sons seekers of the same?

The answer obviously is: teach the word. Teach them when they rise, as you walk with them, as you lie down to sleep – teach, teach, teach. Pray, pray, pray that God will overthrow their plans for marital suicide. Then, if all else fails, do what you can to make their marriage to whomever last and thrive.

But back to our famous lady. What made *her* so special? What did she do that I can emulate?

> *She is like the merchant ships;*
> *She brings her food from afar.*
>
> *She rises also while it is still night,*
> *And gives food to her household;*
> *And portions to her maidens.*
>
> *She considers a field and buys it.*
>
> *– Proverbs 31:14-16a*

It took me some time to read her life with joy rather than embarrassment. It was rather like this to my mind: She rises while it is early. You get up grudgingly. She brings her food from afar. Cooking beans again? She bakes delicious cakes. You use cake mixes.

> *She looks for wool and flax,*
> *And works with her hands in delight.*
>
> *She stretches out her hands to the distaff,*
> *And her hands grasp the spindle.*

She makes coverings for herself;
Her clothing is fine linen and purple.

— Proverbs 31:13,19,22

Worst of all — she sews!!! She works with her hands in *delight,* and her hands grasp the spindle. She makes coverlets for herself; her clothing is of the finest material and color, and she makes linen garments and sells them, etc. I can't sew! Oh, I have tried! (I might make a *cover* for myself but not a dress!)

Maybe God didn't let me be a seamstress because I would have been a greedy one. I would love to be able to make curtains, slip covers, satin, velvet, and lace clothes. I would have been one of those women whose sewing room was always open and the house suffering because I *wanted to sew.* So, God said, "Lea, you teach and write books and buy your clothes on sale." And, that's the way I do.

I would like to have seen those tapestries and the beautiful clothes of purple. She made them herself, not her maidens. She made them by hand. No sewing machine or zippers or straight pins. She went to a lot of trouble to dress well and to have a beautiful home.

Let's take a look at some of her ways. I believe the first thing we would notice about her was her energy. There wasn't a lazy bone in that little lady's body. She had a household to run. There was no way that she could lay in bed because she had servants to feed and to put to work. She was up early and to bed with the lights on at night. No one would have had to call her if something was wrong because she was a light sleeper. "She senses that her gain is good; her lamp does not go out at night" (Proverbs 31:18).

She was a business manager. She knew her job and how to do it. She knew how to feed the clan. She had enough authority from her husband to purchase land for her gardens and vineyards. She made money for such purchases by selling garments and belts to the tradesmen.

She considers a field and buys it;
From her earnings she plants a vineyard.

She makes linen garments and sells them.
And supplies belts to the tradesmen.

— Proverbs 31:16,24

Her family never had to worry about the changing of the seasons because she was ahead of the game. They had boots and gloves and heavy clothes to wear in the cold. (There is no reason today why we cannot do the same no matter what our bank account.) We can have false pride and

14

shun secondhand clothes, but this woman did what was necessary to see that her children and others were warm when it was cold. "She is not afraid of the snow for her household, for all her household are clothed with scarlet" (Proverbs 31:21).

The church here passes their hand-me-downs to the children that are growing up, and they delight to see another child in something that was dear to their own. When God says in Luke 6:38, "Give, and it will be given to you; good measure, pressed down, shaken together, running over, they will pour into your lap," had you ever thought about who the "they" are? Many times it is other Christians sharing with you what they can no longer use. I remember a cousin of mine sending an unexpected huge box of clothes for my little first grade girl when I needed them desperately. God knows our needs and answers them by a "they."

This worthy woman not only saw to her household and their needs, but "she extends her hand to the poor; and she stretches out her hands to the needy" (Proverbs 31:20). I imagine that her leftover clothes or second-hands were to be greatly desired.

Her relationship with her husband was precious. "The heart of her husband trusts in her, and he will have no lack of gain. She does him good and not evil all the days of her life" (Proverbs 31:11). Matthew Henry describes this teaching in this way:

> She is very industrious to recommend herself to her husband's esteem and affection. She conducts herself so that he may repose an entire confidence in her. He trusts in her chastity. He trusts in her conduct, that she will act in all affairs with prudence and discretion. He trusts in her fidelity to his interests. When he goes abroad to attend the concerns of the public, he can confide in her to order all his affairs at home. She contributes so much to his content that he shall have no need of spoil; he needs not to be griping and scraping abroad, as those must be whose wives are proud and wasteful at home. He thinks himself so happy in her that he envies not those who have most of the wealth of the world; he needs it not, he has enough, having such a wife. She shows her love to him, not by a foolish fondness, but by prudent endearments, giving him good words, and not bad ones; no, not when he is out of humour, studying to provide what is fit for him both in health and sickness. And this is her care all the days of her life; not at first only, or now and then, when she is in a good humor, but perpetually. If she survives him, still she is doing him good in her care of his children, his estate and good name.

Surely, her price is above rubies!

DO WE LIKE HER?

We'll never *be* like her if we don't like her. But with God's help and wisdom and our desire to be a worthy woman, we *can* become one. I know that we can! Maybe not as worthy as she was but as worthy as our potential with God's guidance.

And that's not all it says about her husband. "Her *husband* is known in the gates when he sits among the elders of the land" (Proverbs 31:23). She helps him to be an elder. She sees that *his* clothes are up to and above standard.

"Clothes *do* make the man" – and a woman – and her children. Worthy people care about how they look. Her lack of interest in his welfare would have probably kept him from sitting with the elders. Women shame their husbands when their houses are dirty and the clothes unpresentable they wear. We can dress acceptably and in a worthy manner no matter how limited our incomes. But if we are givers, God has promised to supply our needs. *He wants His children to be a proof of His liberality.* When we go out into the public ill-clad, (when we *could* do better), we had better examine our danger of covetousness or our lack of energy and concern for what is best.

"She makes coverings for herself; her clothing is fine linen and purple" (Proverbs 31:22). Purple was the clothing for the rich. Only the rich. This was a king's mother describing the house of the rich Jew. The Jews were at their peak of wealth and of God's blessings. At that time, there were many rich homes.

Was every woman rich? Certainly not. Does every Christian today dress in the finest linen and purple? No, but it isn't wrong to have money or nice clothes. God gives us what is best for us, *and our blessings or lack of them are God-oriented.*

How can we reconcile her clothes with the teaching in 1 Peter? "And let not your adornment be external only – braiding the hair, and wearing gold jewelry, and putting on dresses; but let it be the hidden person of the heart, with the imperishable quality of a gentle and quiet spirit, which is precious in the sight of God" (1 Peter 3:3).

There has been much misteaching on these verses, and there still is.

Many try to make these verses teach that you cannot wear gold. Some even forbid the wearing of a wedding ring. What *is* God saying here? He is saying not to put our *emphasis* on the external – what we wear and how we fix our hair. Now we know that the scripture is not literally saying that we cannot braid our hair or wear any gold. What about the "putting on dresses"? Does God not want women to put on dresses? Is He advocating that we *must* wear slacks? Of course not. Don't stress your looks and what clothing you put on, rather concentrate on a quiet and gentle spirit which is precious to Him.

Is it permissible to wear the purple of the day and to tease my hair? Yes, but always remember where the *emphasis* is – on your heart and not your head and body. Do women have trouble with this? God knows we do. It must be that God teaches us to wear the best that we have when we glorify Him. It is not wrong to dress well, but don't let your heart and soul be bound up in all the trappings. Remember all that is on the earth will burn some day, even the purple and gold.

WHERE WE PUT OUR PRIORITIES

"For where your treasure is, there will your heart be also" (Matthew 6:21).

If your house was on fire, your children safe, and you had a few moments to go and rescue something – what would *you* bring out? Could you stand and watch your clothing, furniture, draperies, and gold be destroyed? Could you stand and thank God that things are as well with you as they are and that all of you are safe? Surely most of us could!

We have a danger in this generation of going to the other extreme. Many well-to-do adults think nothing of appearing in the church assemblies in jeans and sneakers – a current fad. This does not show respect to God or to their fellow men. "Worship the Lord in holy array" (Psalm 29:2).

I remember a gospel preacher, formerly of Alabama, who told of waiting on the Lord's table many years ago in clean overalls and barefooted. That was the best he had. That was the best that many had in the same congregation. *That was his "holy array."*

God loves to show us what He can do for the lives turned over to Him. My mind flits to many different people I have known who started out their Christian lives as very poor people. Then, there began a gradual change for the better: a new job, a better car, a better house and better clothes. As they gave to the Lord, He gave it back "pressed down, shaken together, and running over" (Luke 6:38).

It is one thing to come before the Lord in overalls and barefooted when that is the best you have, than to have a closet full of nice clothes and casually slip into your play or work clothes for worship. The worthy woman saw that her household was well dressed, and she wore purple. And her husband sat with the elders.

WISDOM AND KINDNESS

"She opens her mouth in wisdom and teaching of kindness is on her tongue" (Proverbs 31:26). She wasn't so busy working that she could not teach and teach kindly. She must have had a busy mind that constantly sought ways to improve herself, her family and her community. No one would have been afraid to come to her for advice.

She would have had the spirit of wanting her neighbors and friends to be successful and happy. Jealousy would not have been a part of her makeup. There was no need for her be be jealous, for the blessings of God and her own good works gave her security and self-confidence. Her works worked!

Because she was wise, she could readily see the lack in another and could point out the answer for his or her happiness and success. Any problem is complicated until you have the answer, and then it is simple. I can think of many suggestions made to me through the years by older women. They seem simple now, but they were not before I knew the right way.

PRACTICAL WISDOM

For example, when you rise, make your beds, do your dishes after breakfast, pick up what is out of place. Then, if anyone should come in, there is a semblance of order. Isn't that wise?

Or, before you go to bed at night, straighten up the living room. There might be an emergency in the night and people thronging in. Hide your dishes in the dishwasher if they are unwashed or put a towel over them if there is no dishwasher.

Teach your children when they rise to make up their beds and to pick up after themselves. Rise a little earlier if the time is not adequate. If you teach your children to be tidy, they will stay that way and will not be the kind who delight in destroying others' property. You are raising worthy children. Saturday is the day that their rooms must be cleaned. Each night they have to put away their toys – even preschoolers.

Some may argue, "But *she* had servants!" We do, too – many servants she did not have. We have a washer, dryer, dishwasher, vacuum cleaner, wash-and-wear clothes, hot water, indoor plumbing, and electricity, microwave, and ready made biscuits.

MORE PRACTICAL SUGGESTIONS

You'd like some more ideas from older women? As soon as the children are off to school, plan your supper meal if it is not already planned. Have your rest in the afternoon. Clean up, pretty up, clean up the children, and set the table. When the man walks in, the table is set; he figures that supper is close. (Even if it isn't!)

Make a list of three things you plan to do that day – a reasonable list. Then see that you do them if possible and if not providentially hindered. (We must be able to bend and be flexible.) Be a list maker to be efficient. There are all kinds of lists: grocery, correspondence, and errands to be done. Get a good large datebook.

Wouldn't you just like to follow the worthy woman around with a pad and pencil and learn how much better your life and your family's could be if you had her wisdom?

But, she tells you all these things with kindness, laughing with you at your mistakes instead of "at" you. We agree – "her price is far above rubies."

HER FAMILY'S ESTEEM

"Her children rise up and bless her; her husband also, and he praises her, saying: 'Many daughters have done nobly, but you excel them all' " (Proverbs 31:28,29). Of all people who praise us, whom would we rather hear it from – the world or our family? *Our family knows us.* There are few masks worn in the house. Our family means the most to us. They are bone of our bone. They hold our heart.

When our husband really loves us and admires us and praises us, what more could we ask on earth or as Solomon says "under the sun"? He is our other half; he is the head of this establishment. His praise is the sweetest we ever hear. You know, the boss always knows if the establishment is running right and who is doing the work and who is shirking it. Or he should know.

And her boss said, "You are number one. Many other wives do well, but not as well as you do. I'm blessed that I have you. I love my home. I'm thankful for the way it is run and the way the children look and the way you look. I like to bring guests into our home. You can't be replaced."

And the children say, "Amen." Did you notice that they "rise up" when they bless her. Not a casual looking up from a book and a "Good job, Mom," as they return to their pleasure – but a stopping and rising and a blessing because she deserves it.

God closes the chapter with these words, "Give her the product of her hands and let her works praise her in the gates" (Proverbs 31:31). Why in the gates? Because that is where the people met and talked about the community. When she was praised there, it was evident that the town agreed with her worthiness. No one could rightfully criticize her. Her works praised her, for her works were her proof of industry, wisdom, hard labor, dignity, integrity and concern for those not so blessed as she was.

We, too, rise and bless her and praise her and wipe our eyes and go back to our homes, jobs and responsibilities – but not without hope. For we have seen it done. Our own eyes have registered that it is possible to have such a home. Not only is it possible but desirable. With God's help and wisdom which He has promised to give if we ask, we *will* do better than we have.

We walk away with a fresh determination to improve. Thank you, worthy woman, for being you and for accomplishing the task of running a home and planning and executing the filling of the needs of that home. Thank you for dressing your family and yourself warmly and well, for teaching others with wisdom and kindness, and for sharing your secrets with us.

I just want to touch you.

THOUGHT QUESTIONS

1. What characteristic do you lack that you see in the worthy woman of Proverbs 31?

2. What time do you think the woman of the house should rise?

3. How can we help our sons to look for a worthy woman for marriage, and our daughters be virtuous?

Chapter 3
TO LOVE THEIR HUSBANDS GOD'S WAY

"Let the older women teach, or encourage, or train, or school the younger women to love their husbands."

The first thing — the *very* first thing — is to teach them to love their husbands. This comes first — even before loving their children. Or their parents. Or anybody else. Love HIM. Put him first, for he is number one "under the sun."

Probably older women realize this more than younger women. They live now without their children. They live with that mate, and life is sweeter than it has ever been or worse — if they have lost their husbands along the way and now live with a stranger.

There are more divorces now among the middle-aged than ever before. The children are gone, and the house is quiet. There are no pressing needs, no challenges, no loud music, no hair dryers buzzing, or boys laughing or wrestling, and it is TOO QUIET!

But that wasn't God's plan, and God tries to keep this from happening. "Train them to love their husbands" (Titus 2:4). Teach them to see *that* need. Show them that happiness is a husband who still loves you when the children are gone. This is a challenge!

WHAT DOES A HUSBAND NEED?

God says he *needs* to be respected. "The wife must see to it that she deeply respects her husband — obeying, praising, and honoring him" (L.B.). Another version: "and the woman must see to it that she pays her husband all respect" (N.E.B.) (Ephesians 5:33).

He needs to know that the final say is his on differing opinions. She needs to know this, and the children must know it, too. He is the chief. He is the "house-binder." He is the one whose labor supports the family.

He is the lifeline for food, clothing, sustenance, love, and direction. Teach the children that HE comes first. "Dad will be home soon. We need to clean up and look nice. Pick up your things because Dad likes for the house to look nice. He has worked hard, so don't go dumping on him your unhappiness."

Serve him first. Serve him his favorite piece of chicken. You are teaching your children to honor their parents. It used to be that the kids "took a cold tater and waited" until the adults were served. Now, the papa is lucky if the neck is still on the plate by the time it gets to him. *That's not right.*

Send the children from the table if they cannot behave or stop crying or yelling or whatever. This is PRIME TIME, and the children must be taught this. The world should not revolve or turn around our children but our husbands. (And already some mother is mad at me for such teaching.)

The prayer is said. The father is served and then the children. Food is not piled on their plates to be thrown out after picked over. Put a little of everything on their plates, and no "I don't like" or "Yuk" is allowed. Teach them the food has been provided by God and is to be eaten with thanksgiving. With this process, the children in time will learn to like all foods. And parents will not have to hear constant tears and disturbances at the table. (A lot of this is pretaught before the meal by the mother.) This is *family* time.

WHAT DOES A MAN WANT IN A WIFE?

I was reading the result of a survey made asking this question, and they found that the men in these 1980's want the same thing men wanted in the 80 B.C.'s – "simple compatibility, dependability and a pleasing disposition."

Men want to come home to a sweet wife, a cheerful wife, a clean wife, and a happy wife. Her attitude is *so* important. Really, it sets the stage for the family. If Mama has a good sense of humor, there is a continual feast in the house. "All the days of the afflicted are bad, but a cheerful heart has a continual feast" (Proverbs 15:15).

Washington Irving said it like this. "Honest good humor is the oil and wine of a merry meeting, and there is no jovial companionship equal to that where the jokes are rather small, and the laughter abundant."

(Children seem to naturally have a good sense of humor. Have you ever noticed when you watch cartoons with them that you laugh at the same things? When our family gets together for a reunion, most of the time is spent retelling funny situations that happened in the past. And we tell the same things each time and laugh again.)

The survey also found that "despite women's lib" the men polled didn't want their mates to be big bread winners – just loving companions.

22

Men need to be loved and loved and loved. They may not even know they need it, but they do. We need to be touchers with our husbands and with our children. Touch often. *Someone has to start the touching,* and most times it is the wives. Babies can die without it and so can marriages.

YOU ARE NOT GOING TO CHANGE HIM

"A woman marries with the idea of changing her husband as well as her name. A man marries under the illusion his bride will stay the same" – Walsh.

Only God can change us. We cannot change others and can only change ourselves gradually with God's help and our cooperation. We are all born with some inherited traits. Read Tim LaHaye's *Understanding the Male Temperament or What Every Man Would Like to Tell His Wife About Himself, but Won't.*

He suggests it is a person's born temperament that makes him outgoing and extrovertish or shy and introvertish. He says, "Humanly speaking nothing has as much influence on your behavior than your inherited temperament."

Our environment, too, has a lasting impression and influence on our lives. We have picked neither our parents or our neighborhoods, and we suffer or are blessed by the same. Someone has said, "As the twig is bent so the tree is inclined to grow." We are both pretty "bent" by the time we are old enough to marry.

I read a shocking statement that said a criminal is formed by the time he is three. I hope that is untrue. I have read that fifty percent of a child's character is formed by the time he is three, and seventy-five percent by the time he is five. And this husband of ours is in his twenties or more.

This is why it is so important to marry in the Lord because you do not have two people wanting to live as their natural lives demand, rather two people hopefully who have died to self and are in the hands of God to be shaped into new creatures. Remember "we are by nature children of wrath" (Ephesians 2:3).

Good husbands are made, not born and so are good wives and mothers. What leverage is there for change when you are married to a non-Christian who cares not what the Scriptures say? The changes are lopsided.

I have personally seen young Christian husbands who would never think of grabbing a broom changed by seeing a godly elder do any job that needs to be done in the house.

What about a marriage where the husband has been raised wrong and has seemingly a bad natural temperament? Can anything be done? We all know that "with God all things are possible." "A person who *wants* to

23

change, to start anew, can change, but it will not be an overnight process. And the desire must come from within himself. *You* can be the greatest human help he has. "In whatever yoke you find yourself, pray for wisdom to know how to do your part wisely" – Tim LaHaye.

"A mature man is one who is sufficiently objective about himself to know both his strengths and his weaknesses. No one needs to be conquered by his weaknesses" – Anonymous.

DOES GOD SHOW ME HOW
TO LOVE
MY HUSBAND?

Of course all of our answers to this life and the one to come are in the Book. God shows us how to love. *God is love,* and we cannot continue to look at Him without looking like Him and loving like Him.

God knows how important our sexual needs are, and He spells out part of this needed action in 1 Corinthians 7:3-5.

> *The husband should give to his wife her conjugal rights, and likewise the wife to her husband. For the wife does not rule over her own body, but the husband does. Do not refuse one another except by agreement for a season, that you might devote yourselves to prayer. But then come together again lest Satan tempt you through lack of self-control.*

Marriage counselors advise troubled married couples to continue their sexual relationship. You grow farther apart when one leaves the marriage bed. Sex is a need, and when we *stop* fulfilling that need, there is a danger that others will fulfill it.

Christian wives should be giving wives. A leading women's magazine sponsored a survey about women and their love lives and found out (probably to their surprise) that religious women were the most giving in their sexual relationships.

A good sexual life is a learned art and a gift from God. I really believe that. I think God wants us to be happy even sexually or why would He spell out the instructions that He does concerning sex?

There again, our environment and our parental examples and teachings often mar our marriages rather than enhance them. But we can *learn* everything that is needed, and God will give us wisdom even in this – *if we ask Him.*

Tim LaHaye says, "If he and his bride wed with the approval of his parents and no animosity exists in his heart, he can with loving consideration, proper reading, and/or counseling, become a good lover." Why can't a woman do the same thing?

If God tells us to love each other and enjoy each other, won't He help us? "Enjoy life with the woman whom you love all the days of your fleeting life, which He has given you under the sun. For this is your reward in life, and in your toil in which you have labored under the sun" (Ecclesiastes 9:9).

NON-SEXUAL LOVE

Women have to teach their husbands the value of non-sexual love. At first in the honeymoon days when a wife reaches for her husband in kissing or touching or hugging, he thinks she is reaching for him in a sexual way.

However, the time comes when he must understand that often she is just wanting to be held or cuddled, and that's all. Growing up in a family, we had times we wanted to be touched by our family, and those were good times. We have the same feeling for our husbands, and we can help them remember the loving times they had with their own families. (Our grown daughters still occasionally plop themselves on our laps – we like it!!)

My heart goes out to the old people in the nursing home who want someone to just touch them. They want to be hugged and noticed and spoken to warmly. *We never outgrow our need as humans to be touched.*

Touching says a lot of things. It says, "You are special, and I want you to know it." It says, "You are not one of the cold world out there, but you are family." It says, "I belong to you, and you belong to me." It says, "You sure look nice this morning all clean shaven and smelling of lotion and soap." It says, "Take care of yourself because you can't be replaced." It says, like that old nursery game we used to play, "I measure my love to show you." It says, "You're mine, and I'm glad!"

Now all that needs to be said! Right? And often! And the more you say it, the deeper the encounter.

"Touch Me"

Touch me in the morning when the night still clings,
at midday when confusion crowds around me,
in the evening when I see and hear you best of all,
and at night when I can't see you but I know you
are there.

Touch me with your hands but also with your eyes,
with your words, with your thoughts,
with your presence in my room.

Touch me like a child who is strong enough to give,
like a mother who has brought life into this world,
like a father whose gnarled and calloused hands
often touch things instead of people.
Touch me when I ask you to and
Touch me when I'm afraid to ask you to.
Touch me gently, I'm so fragile.
Touch me firmly, for I'm so strong, but most importantly,
Touch me often, for without your touch, I'm so alone.

— Marriage Encounter

LEARN TO LOVE
THE LITTLE BOY IN HIM

It takes time to appreciate the fact that a young husband has to have time to learn it all. He has to learn how to lead, how to make a living, how to love his wife and children, how to have the right answers, how to grow up, and how to face his responsibilities.

A wife's demands can discourage him into depression. More men commit suicide than women. More men walk out on their wives than wives walk out on their husbands.

Most young women do not admire or want the little boy who lives in their husbands. Rather, they want the strength and security they found in their own fathers. Too often she wants to start out marriage with the things that have taken her parents over 20 years to acquire — and that includes patience and maturity. (Many of those years were spent in doing without and eking a living just as she will probably have to do in her own young marriage.)

So, when her husband wants to be with the boys, or foolishly wants to waste their living on sports or entertainment that they cannot afford, she panics.

Many older women know a secret that they can share with the younger. Learn to love that little boy if you want *him* to love *you* with all his heart. Read the book *To Understand Each Other* by Dr. Paul Tournier. He suggests that we talk often about our husband's childhood with him and then LISTEN. Talk about his pets, his hurts, his defeats, and happinesses, and as he answers, he gives you *himself*. The more he shares his boyhood with you, the less he would ever consider leaving you.

Spend hours talking about his youth — you are learning to communicate. He learns to trust you as he reveals his longings that were fulfilled or unfulfilled, his past justices or injustices, his loves and his hates, his successes and his failures. *Remember he is giving you himself.*

26

And the beautiful part about it is that you are discovering the *real* him. You are learning how to appreciate his ways and his reactions and his deep desires for the future. You are learning to love him more. Notice how a man delights in seeing his baby pictures and hearing over and over the things he used to do. (You like those things, too – don't you?) Think how close we came to not knowing the love that we can now share because we did not know how important his "little boy" was and is! Strange as it may seem, this is part of a "wise woman building her house" (Proverbs 14:1).

HE WON'T TALK TO ME

I know that women are puzzled to find that the man who called her every day, talked for hours while courting, and who wouldn't bring her home without sitting and talking until daylight – *now won't talk!!*

What happened? There have been libraries of books written to diagnose this mysterious disease, and what makes *me* think I have the answers when we are still working on the problem ourselves? (Presumptious, I'd say.) I doubt that it is as important to know *why* it has happened as it is to know how to fix it or cure it.

Probably the first reason for the steady talking changing to silence is that the man's role has changed from winning a wife to supporting one. It is hard to make a good living. (It is a lot harder than courting.) It is hard, and yet it is a challenge. Many men become workaholics because of the challenge. There is competition, and men usually like some of that, especially if they are winning. A charge has been put upon them to support their families' needs.

"But if anyone does not provide for his own, and especially those of his household he has denied the faith and is worse than an unbeliever" (1 Timothy 5:8).

It has to be a scary proposition to know that it falls on him to feed, clothe, and supply a house for his family. It falls on his shoulders to take care of transportation, schooling, extra training for himself, and getting his family to heaven.

He comes in tired. More tired than we realize if we have never worked away from home. He made it through the door. He hopes to make it across the room to his chair, and we say prettily, "Let's talk awhile."

We have been in the house with the "wreckers," and he has come in from the exciting outside. Things have been happening in *his* world. An adult has walked in. We often don't see a bone-tired individual, but rather we see the handsome man who left this morning and whom we have thought about all day and anticipated his arrival. Here's my companion, my co-worker, my lover – Hallelujah!! (And he may even think in his youthful

27

way, "I'd feel like she does too, if I had been home all day, had a nap, had time to shower and fix up. And if I'd done nothing harder than open a few cans and do a little babysitting.") This kind of thinking does *not* open up to pleasant communication.

This is emergency time. What can I do to make it better? What does he want me to do? He probably doesn't *know* what he wants you to do. Follow his lead. You will learn in time what he needs. Be a geisha girl.

He may not only be tired, he may be depressed. Someone has said that the thing that worries a man most of all is the threat of failure. He may be and probably is worried and depressed. What will he do if he can't pay the rent? You *have* to pay the rent. Where is there anyone to help? Should he encourage the wife to go out and work and leave the children so that he won't have to worry as he now is? Everybody else's wife is working. *Their* kids are surviving.

(The other day on a talk show on TV a lot of time was spent on the supposed advantage of women leaving home and children for the development of a career. One woman asked, "What do you do when your husband demands that you work, and you want to be at home?" No one had an answer.)

Maybe it is best that he doesn't talk when he first comes in. The evening is going to get better. He is going to eat and enjoy his meal and his family. Bedtime for the young ones is not far away, and there will be a quiet time together — unless he is hooked on escapism: television, the newspaper, books, or hobbies. If so, we are going to have to learn to adapt to his schedule. Maybe in time, he will begin to love communication and seek it on his own, but I doubt it.

God told the *women* to adapt to their husbands. They are to be the adapters. If he wants to watch TV, watch it with him. Go and sit with him. (You can talk during the commercials.) If he wants to read, get your book and read. If he wants to go out occasionally with his bowling buddies and you don't like to bowl, see if you can find a hobby with others. Usually when he comes in from a night out, he is in a talking mood. You can have some snacks ready and make this the time to get reacquainted. TIMING IS SO IMPORTANT. Pray for wisdom to know when it is the time for talking. Have something funny to tell him that the kids said or did or something about the neighbors. Talk to him about the news — keep up with the news. Be an interesting conversationalist. Talk about what he likes to talk about, and in time *you* will be his favorite listener. Home will be better than anywhere else because *you* are there, and you know him and understand him.

Ask him what happened on the job and let him pour out his joys and dissatisfactions. Use your home and table to entertain his workers if he would like that. Get into his world, and the talk will eventually come about. Listen lovingly and be interested in what he is saying. Learn to understand even what he is *not* saying that is important. Teach him to talk by loving him and listening. As a result, the communication flows; your relationship with him grows deeper and stronger; and above all, you become good friends.

ARRANGE SPECIAL DATES

Here is a quote from a recent newspaper:

> Women have affairs because they want better communication and more emotional support. Women aren't after 'extra sex and variety' when they have an affair. What they do want is a more satisfying relationship.

God's women *must* be smarter than this.

It will be a wise young woman who knows from the first that there should be a once-a-week-time to go out together. It doesn't have to be an expensive evening. McDonald's still lives. It may be planning a time to drop by and be with another couple after eating out. It may be driving around together or going out to the lake or ocean, or whatever is beautiful in your world. But, dress up and get out and have the feeling of the good old days when you were dating.

If you are a little older and have more money, go to a motel carrying a new nightgown. Get away from the telephone and the pressures of your every day life. If you do not have a competent babysitter, then start a swapping program with friends so that you can have the night off. DON'T LET GO OF YOUR ROMANCE! Getting completely away is wonderful. Put your good mind to the challenge of arranging this. You don't have to stay at the best motel if you can't afford it – it is the getting away together that is so important – not where you went. Make it an adventure!

You can have a special time together each night when he is home. Use your living room for living. Be close to him as you sit together. Have snacks available during the evening. Teach the children that you two like to have a little time together each evening as they play in the family room or bedroom. Provide for them a small TV, record player, books, colors, etc. And when they come running in and demanding something, teach them that this is Dad and Mom's time together. They will soon learn. Don't let the kids run the institution.

Then at bedtime, *both* of you should put the kids to bed. A joint endeavor. At first he may resent this interruption, but in time he will look forward to it. The children will have lasting memories of the security they felt at the end of each day. And they will not forget it.

Try not to have spankings and upsets at bedtime. Outsmart the kids – a drink, the bathroom and to bed, after their prayers.

Incidentally, do not allow the children to stay up late. They need the rest – *you* need the rest from *them*.

Many marriages are hurt because of "everlasting" children. Foolishness is bound in the hearts of children, and parents, too, have an attention span!

DON'T BE BORING

When you read these past few thoughts, it may seem like I am suggesting that you be completely passive with no thoughts or a mind of your own. *We cannot always adapt to every whim of his!* There are times that we have to acknowledge that we are two different people with thoughts of our own and even differing convictions.

I've heard people say, "We have never had an argument or disagreement." If that is true, then someone is always giving in, and that is not honest. In really getting to know each other, we gradually learn what we differ on. No one is always right.

Husbands are human, and most of them are given to logic. They work out in the world where they often disagree with the boss and their fellow workers. Yet they still admire them and stay friends.

I believe that most men admire a woman who is strong and can think for herself and can make differing judgments. I don't think most men want to be married to a whiny wimp – yessir, whatever you say, sir. There are a few men who *need* such a wife, but most men don't.

Don't *love* to disagree and deliberately unhinge him. But also do not be afraid to express your opinions, for the two becoming one *has* to be an honest relationship.

We remember Sarah telling her husband to put the concubine and her son out of the house, out to fend for themselves, out with no friends or way of sustaining themselves and Abraham refused. God said in essence, "She's right. Do it. It is time now to regroup and time for trouble to leave your home." (God said that Ishmael and his mother would be taken care of).

God put Sarah up for our example in 1 Peter 3, and He says to look at her and emulate her. She was a loving wife and a delight to Abraham the whole time that she lived. She was an adapter but *not* passive.

FORGET THE FUSSES OF YESTERDAY

Today will have enough evil of its own. Learn from the past disagreements, but forget the words said. Passion says a lot of things it doesn't mean and wishes it had not said.

We don't have yesterday's strength — only today's. Forgive and forget. You will only destroy yourself by harboring the mistakes. God tells us to forget the things that are behind.

Someone has said, "A happy marriage is one that begins anew every day." Another said, "A successful marriage requires falling in love many times with the same person."

Marriage is not to be endured but enjoyed, and we can't enjoy it if we are smarting over past offenses. Talk it out. If you cannot handle it inwardly, then handle it outwardly. Forebear or handle it.

God teaches us to be a forbearing people, and one definition for forbearance is "restraining from action." Can you overlook the action, forgive it, consider it unimportant — or is it too big? Must you bring it out in the open? If you must, *do it*, talk it out, and then forget it.

God tells us to not go to sleep at night until we have fixed our anger problem. Sometimes that is hard to do, especially when we are right, and they won't talk about it but go to sleep. What then? It probably wasn't big to them, and they have forgiven and forgotten. Maybe sleeping on it will make us realize too, that it really wasn't that big. (It usually isn't.) But sometimes it is, and there must come a clearing time — an air clearing time — so *both* parties can sleep the next night.

Remember that two imperfect people are living together raising imperfect children. Battles are bound to be fought, but there must not be a war where either one no longer chooses to have a truce but decides to part and stay enemies. Again we come back to communication. We *have* to make marriage so wonderful for each other that we cannot live the day until we are back fighting for each other instead of against each other. *This household must stand if possible!*

THE HONEYMOON IS OVER

We don't "love" each other as we used to. The excitement is gone. It's down to the nitty gritty, and we both want out!! We want to find a new love.

America is bombarded with sexual misinformation. Novels, TV, and magazines tell us of fictionalized romances that never die, and we believe them because we want to.

There is a very good book to read on the realism of "falling in love." It is called *The Road Less Traveled* and is written by M. Scott Peck, M.D. He says:

> We fall in love only when we are consciously or unconsciously sexually motivated. The second problem is that the experience of falling in love is invariably temporary. No matter whom we fall in

love with, we sooner or later fall out of love if the relationship con-
tinues long enough. This is not to say that we invariably cease lov-
ing the person with whom we fell in love. But it is to say the feeling
of ecstatic lovingness that characterizes the experience of falling in
love always passes. The honeymoon always ends. The bloom of
romance always fades.

– Pages 84,85

Forty-five years ago I remember reading an article by Dorothy Dix (the Dear Abby of yesterday). She said that changing mates is just changing one set of faults for another.

Older men who swap their wives for younger ones are just chasing the wind. The new honeymoon won't last either. If the put away wife could get her hurt under control and wait, he will usually be back.

THE ANSWERS

What's the answer then? We are all vulnerable to real love. Falling in love is a matter of choice and temporary. Real love grows and develops into maturity. We never have too much love – love that acts whether it feels like it or not.

Dr. Peck says that "love is a form of work or a form of courage . . . But since it requires the extension of ourselves, love is always either work or courage. If an act is not one of work or courage, then it is not an act of love. There are no exceptions" (p. 120).

Assuming this to be true and realizing that agape love is a decision – "I will love you no matter what you do or say" – then what do we do to make our marriage work after the honeymoon is over? We maturely and with God's wisdom build our own worthy woman's home. We follow the pattern given. We set out to make our husband a home like hers, and hap-piness comes to us inadvertently, *a by-product.*

DOES YOUR HUSBAND HAVE
A GOOD MARRIAGE?

If he does, you have succeeded in the job God has given you. If he does not, then keep working and endeavoring for that goal.

Some wife protests, "But what about *me* and *my happiness?* Isn't something put on *him* to satisfy me?"

Yes. God wants the Christian man to try to please his wife. Paul writes, "but one who is married is concerned about the things of the world, how he may please his wife, and his interests are divided" (1 Corinthians 7:33,34a). "Husbands, love your wives, just as Christ also loved the church and gave Himself up for her . . ." (Ephesians 5:25).

Listen to 1 Peter 3:7-9:

> *You husbands likewise, live with your wives in an understanding way, as with a weaker vessel, since she is a woman; and grant her honor as a fellow-heir of the grace of life, so that your prayers may not be hindered. To sum up, let all be harmonious, sympathetic, brotherly, kindhearted, and humble in spirit; not returning evil for evil, or insult for insult, but giving a blessing instead; for you were called for the very purpose that you might inherit a blessing.*

Both parties are "to follow after the things that make for peace" (Romans 14:19). God ever sees and records all who do, or do not do, their part as Christians in the marriage.

The burden or challenge, depending on the wife's attitude, still falls on her to build the house, and the house usually rises or falls on her wisdom or lack of wisdom in building.

DO YOU HAVE A GOOD MARRIAGE?

Very seldom would the woman prefer living alone to living with him. Though sometimes it is *that bad* in some relationships.

God recognizes this in 1 Corinthians 7:11: (but if she does leave, let her remain unmarried, or else be reconciled to her husband), and that the husband should not send his wife away. However, we must wisely consider that we do not jump from the frying pan into the fire.

Our attitude can usually better whatever the existing situation. We need to count our blessings. We must grow to be mature. We must not be the foolish woman who tears down her own house.

The lesson of Abigail can help us. Though her husband, Nabal, was churlish and rude, she still was admired and served by her household as she strove to serve and respect her husband. Leaving her home and husband would have left her homeless and unprotected. God gave her a happy ending. Remember Hagar's observance when God sent an angel to her in her predicament. She said, "God sees" (Genesis 16:13).

WHAT CAUSES DIVORCE?

In one word — immaturity. In another word — selfishness. In one word or more — lack of knowledge of God's words for happiness. "I Did it My Way" is the theme song for this generation.

God says, "It is not in man to direct his own steps" (Jeremiah 10:23).

God says, "Every man's way is right in his own eyes" (Proverbs 21:2).

God says, "Do not lean on your own understanding . . . Do not be wise in your own eyes" (Proverbs 3:5,7).

God says, "Do unto others as you would have them do unto you" (Matthew 7:12).

God says, "Seek ye first the kingdom of God and His righteousness; and all these things shall be added unto you" (Matthew 6:33).

We marry in our youth. We move away from our parents and their wisdom and care. We are free — free to make our own wrong decisions. Free to practice the mistakes of youth and free from having to give an accounting for our actions. Free from wisdom, free from knowledge of what is right and proper. Free to demand our own way.

Hopefully, we have been instilled with character and good examples from our parents. We have been disciplined and know what is right and wrong, and our consciences burn within us as we leave the old paths of righteousness and rules.

In time we will do as it says in Psalm 22:6, "Train up a child in the way he should go, even when he is old he will not depart from it."

Tim LaHaye says, "Character is not born within a person. It is formed into him by loving and concerned parents who will establish within his life those principles which God has instilled within their own."

But what if we have married in our immaturity the one whose parents have not instilled these good qualities and teachings? Then, I must double up on my Bible knowledge and practice and teach by example the way for him. (We are all ever vulnerable to our parents and environment.) We must also double up on our prayer life, asking for wisdom.

It is so easy to divorce. It is no longer shocking to the world. The time may come when our mate no longer desires our love and presence. He may chafe at our longing to please God and desires to continue to do it his way. He may leave or find another. Now we understand what 2 Corinthians 6:14-18 was trying to tell us.

> Do not be bound together with unbelievers; for what partnership have righteousness and lawlessness, or what fellowship has light with darkness? Or what harmony has Christ with Belial, or what has a believer in common with an unbeliever? Or what agreement has the temple of God with idols? For we are the temple of the living God; just as God said,

I will dwell in them and walk among them;
And I will be their God, and they shall be my people.
Therefore, come out from their midst and be separate,
  says the Lord.

And do not touch what is unclean;
And I will welcome you.
And I will be a father to you,

And you shall be sons and daughters to me,
says the Lord.

Through our tears and heartbreak we find that God knew what He was saying.

But, no matter what, God can pick up the pieces and show us that life is not over, and we will live again more wisely.

WHEN DO I BEGIN TO WORRY ABOUT US?

1. When sexual advances begin to diminish in a young man.
2. When we habitually retire at different times.
3. When one keeps putting the other one down publicly.
4. When one or both begin to think divorce is a possible alternative.

SOME PRACTICAL AND CONSTRUCTIVE ADVICE

Look as good as you can. Dress as well as possible. Learn to cover up what your figure lacks. Read magazines that help. Learn to pick the colors that look best on you; learn how to fix your hair, and learn what makeup is best. Be clean – Abby says a woman can't take too many baths. Use perfume that he likes.

Tell him how attractive you are. Don't ever point out your double chin or whatever. He might not have noticed it before. (When you tell him, he will always notice it.) I remember hearing a true story of a lady who always exchanged her husband's Christmas gift of lingerie. He always bought her something beautiful that was a size 12, and she exchanged it for a larger size with nothing said. If he thought she still wore a size 12, who was she to correct him?

Let him know often – daily – that you admire his masculinity. "The two things that fracture the male ego most quickly are threats to his masculinity and fear of sexual inadequacy" – La Haye. He needs to know that he is an attractive man, and he needs to hear it from *you* most of all!

You married him by your own choice. You see an attraction others may not. (I really feel that my husband is probably the most attractive man in the room! He knows I feel that way because I tell him. I tell him just by looking at him. I help dress *him* to look his best.)

Touch him with non-sexual love and with sexual love. Kiss in the elevator (assuming that you two are alone). Always pick the table in the restaurant dining room that enables you to talk privately and cozily.

Always know where he is in a crowded room. Be looking for him as he looks for you, and let your eyes light up when you see him. Write down ten things you like about your husband, and thank God each day for those same things. Tell him often of his good points. Show your love for him in front of others. "Come and sit by me." Are you conscious of the women with happy marriages that you know? What do they think about *your* marriage?

Learn to be content in whatever state you are in – whatever house, whatever car, whatever clothes, whatever pay check, etc. He deserves praise for doing as well as he does. *Your respect is his number one need.* Don't forget that! Have sympathy for his role as provider for as long as you both shall live. Would you want that responsibility placed on you?

God did not make wives to be in competition with their husbands. Rather, after the fall, God said, "Your desire will be to your husband" or as one version says, "Your desire will be to please your husband" (Genesis 3:16). That is a gift from God to both of the marriage partners. *God wants peace in the home.* He tells the woman to please her husband, and he tells the husband to not be bitter against his wife.

Have you ever heard the story about the wife who went to her lawyer and said she wanted a divorce because she hated her husband? She was only sorry that she could not think of something really bad to do to him before she left him for good. Her lawyer suggested a devious plan. He said, "Make him need you, and when you are gone, you can walk out laughing, and he will be crying."

So, she did this. She became his slave – anything to please him. She worked at it, for she was a clever woman. Several months later she ran into the lawyer, and he asked if it was time to file the papers. And she said incredulously, "You think I'd leave that wonderful man?" She learned how to please her husband, and it resulted in him wanting to please her. They both fell in love again in the process. As she treated him as a king, he in turn realized he had a queen!

IN CONCLUSION

Your husband needs you more than he needs any other person on earth. You are his woman, his mate, his other half, his friend, companion, lover – all that he lacked is in you. Find your niche in the circle of his arms. Hold onto him while you have him, for statistics say that you will outlive him ten years. The time will come when you wish you could pick up his dirty socks, or could find the toothpaste squeezed from the top, or could hear him driving in from work, or hear his voice calling on the phone, or find a card that you reminded him to buy that said "Happy Anniversary," or remember the Christmas Eves when he ran out at the last minute to get your present.

Or know you will never hear him say again, "There's never a time that you touch me day or night that I don't know it" or "I've always been fierce about you."

Hug him while you have him, for ten years is a long time to be alone.

THOUGHT QUESTIONS

1. What is a husband's greatest need from a wife?
2. Name the two kinds of touchings needed.
3. What can I do to keep or start communication?
4. What kind of love does a good marriage need?

Chapter 4
TO LOVE OUR CHILDREN ENOUGH

"Mother's Prayer"

Oh give me patience when wee hands
Tug at me with their small hands
And give me gentle and smiling eyes.
Keep my lips from hasty replies.
And let not weariness, confusion, or noise
Obscure my vision of life's fleeting joys.
So when, in years to come my house is still –
No bitter memories its room may fill.

– Anonymous

God teaches in an orderly way. First, He tells the older women to teach the younger women to love their husbands, for this relationship is the key relationship. The love for each other is the foundation of the new marriage. It takes three to make a Christian marriage: God, the husband, and the wife. It takes the same three to bring up Christian children and mold them into Christian adults.

Under the old law, God gave the honeymooners a year to get acquainted after the marriage vows were said. The man had the year off – a year to learn to know his wife, her needs, her wants, her strengths, and her weaknesses. A year to begin to lead and to feel responsible for his wife. A year for her to love to be the "held" and not the "head."

The wheel took the men away from their homes and into the factories. The computer helps to hold him there. It used to be that most men were around the house night and day. They were a part of birthing, living, and dying, and all that is in between. (Divorce statistics teach us that *was* the better way.)

FATHERS, WHERE ARE YOU?

God said, "And, fathers, do not provoke your children to anger; but bring them up in the discipline and instruction of the Lord" (Ephesians 6:4) (RSV). We tend to emphasize the first part of this verse and ignore the second part. "You (fathers) bring them up in the discipline and instruction of the Lord." Bring them up from the cradle to their wedding day with all of the discipline and instruction that they need.

God says, "Bring them up" – or "Train up a child" and He gives explicit instructions on how to go about it (Deuteronomy 6:6-9:

> *And these words, which I am commanding you today, shall be on your heart; and you shall teach them diligently to your sons and shall talk of them when you sit in your house and when you walk by the way and when you lie down and when you rise up. And you shall bind them as a sign on your hand and they shall be as fron-tals on your forehead. And you shall write them on the doorposts of your house and on your gates.*

Talk to them four times: when you sit in the house, when you walk out of the house, when you lie down, and when you get up. That just about covers your waking hours and locations. *Talk, talk, talk.* Talk in season and out of season – when they want to hear it and when they don't.

Children are going to grow up – age wise – but that doesn't mean they were *brought* up. As the old saying from *Uncle Tom's Cabin,* "Topsy just grew." She had no *raising.*

Children tend to listen to their fathers more – they take them more seriously than they do their mothers. Their voices are deeper; they are big-ger and more impressive in appearance, and they tend to be sterner. Dads don't fool around and usually don't give the instructions as often as Mamas do before they take action.

(When will we ever learn that when God speaks, it is not *just* for in-struction, but it also is to tell us that this is the ONLY way that things work? God doesn't go into detail; He just says, *"Do it this way."* It takes us a long time to learn that this is the ONLY way.")

"Fathers, do not exasperate your children, that they may not lose heart" (Colossians 3:21). This instruction is not given to mothers. Why? Because mothers put up with a lot more from the kids. We want peace quicker. We often get in the way of the father's discipline. This shows, too, we are the weaker vessel. Many times we force the husband into "disciplining" us before he can get to the child. We "save" the child from deserved and

40

needed chastenings. Don't we, Mamas?

Before we get too hard on the mothers, we must in all fairness say that most fathers of today do not know their children like their mothers do. They are gone all day, and they come in bone-tired and weary. The wives feel responsible for the children's misbehavior and for their noisy ways. They want the husband to be "protected" from his children, and most men want this, too. So, he yells at the kids, and maybe in anger spanks them hastily and bedlam is here. (As my little granddaughter says, "I'm in berserk.") And in "berserk" is the household when there was such high hopes of joy at Dad's return.

HOW TO REALLY LOVE YOUR CHILD

This is the name of a book written by Dr. Ross Campbell. Get that book! It is the best advice I have ever read by a father on child raising. Fathers are failing God and their wives and most of all, their children when they do not realize and obey what God instructs them to do.

Dr. Campbell says:

1. "A husband's willingness to be completely answerable for his family is one of the greatest assets a wife and child can have."

2. "The husband must take the responsibility for initiating love. It is hard at first but will become easy."

3. "The love returned to him by his wife is the most precious commodity in the world."

4. "I have never seen a marriage fail where the husband took full, total, overall responsibility for his family and took the initiative in conveying his love to his wife and children."

God says it this way:

You wives must learn to adapt yourselves to your husbands as you submit yourselves to the Lord, for the husband is the head of the wife in the same way that Christ is the head of the church and the Saviour of the body. The willing subjection of the church to Christ should be reproduced in the submission of wives to their husbands in everything. The husband must give his wife the same sort of love that Christ gave to the church when he sacrificed himself for her. So men ought to give their wives the love they naturally have for their own bodies. The love a man gives his wife is the extending of his love for himself to enfold her . . . In practice what I have said amounts to this: let every one of you who is a hus-

band love his wife as he loves himself, and let every wife respect her husband.

— Ephesians 5:25-33 (Phillips)

Questions: Do most husbands understand these charges given to them? Does the wife? Will he accept them? How can he oversee the house and lead in love when he is not there? Can we hope for the man to show tender love and affection for his wife and children when he comes home after 12 to 14 hours of hard labor, and the children whom he left in bed are now back in bed? How can the wife encourage his lead and discipline of the children when he does not know them? Have you ever seen a home where this ideal is practiced — the man in the loving lead and the wife and children reflecting this love and security?

Although God has taught us the correct way to run a Christian home, we realize that the ideal is still to be accomplished. We can work and pray for the ideal, but we can be comforted with the realization that *God will help us raise our children in whatever circumstances we find ourselves.* We learn to be a team. We start out knowing little or nothing about raising children, and our hearts' desire is to raise them into responsible, worthy adults who bring glory to the name of Christ.

LET'S TALK ABOUT BABIES

"Little Human Blossoms"

Flowers, I love flowers, and I'll say that they are sweet,
But no flower has got pink toes, on a pair of rose leaf feet.
And no flower has got arms, that go up round a fellow's neck.
And no flower ever whispers that it love you 'most a peck.
And no flower is so wearied when the long play day is by
That it snuggles to your bosom, almost ready to cry,
Till you start to count the piggies. I love flowers, they are fine,
But it's little human blossoms that have touched this heart of mine.

It's the little human blossoms that can holler and can run,
With their arms upheld to greet you when your working day is done,
That your eyes begin to look for when you turn into the street
And your ears begin to listen for the patter of their feet,
That makes your arms reach out to hold them and your face break into smiles
Oh, it's little human blossoms that makes glad life's weary miles!
And the bluest morning glory, its rare blossoms gemmed with dew,
Ain't as pretty as a baby with its arms held up to you.

I know a lot of millionaires, I know about them anyhow,
I know their very presence makes man start to scrape and bow
But I never envy them none − they don't have the things I seek,
Dollars can't climb in your arms and hold their cheek against your cheek
Like a baby can, and love you. Dollars seem plum cheap and cold
When they are put beside a baby that your arms can lift and hold.
Millions are not necessary. Roses may not climb your wall
But life without little human blossoms ain't worth anything at all.

− Anonymous

As we go through the valley of the shadow, the remembrance of the pain fades when we see that little face. "Whenever a woman is in travail she has sorrow, because her hour has come; but when she gives birth to the child, she remembers the anguish no more, for joy that a child has been born into the world" (John 16:21).

God says a baby is a gift from Him. "Behold children are a gift of the Lord. The fruit of the womb is a reward. Like arrows in the hand of a war-rior, so are the children of one's youth. How blessed is the man whose quiver is full of them, they shall not be ashamed" (Psalm 127:3,4).

He often gives them to women who are barren. "He makes the barren woman abide in the house as a joyful mother of children. Praise the Lord" (Psalm 113:9).

The bride who slept till noon now jumps up when the baby sneezes or coughs. When the baby cries, she thinks he is dying, and when he has stopped crying, she is afraid he's gone.

Much is being learned about babies that didn't used to be known. Babies know their mother's heartbeat and recognize her voice before birth. They need bonding and love and touching from day one, or they can die from lack of it.

The natural way was the home birth with all of the family there, and many are going back to this. The natural way was nursing, and we are learning now there are immunities from disease present with the benefits of nursing as well as fewer fat cells to plague us as adults. The most impor-tant part of nursing is that the two of you get to know each other. You *have* to sit down or lie down and rest and talk to each other. (If you *must* bottle feed, still take this time to hold them and get acquainted. How I wish an older woman had taught me this.)

God expects the mother to do the holding − to be at home with her babies. Even Dr. Salk says that mothers should be with their preschoolers. Don't fall for this new psychology that the child will do just as well with a substitute. No matter how well a child seems to do with another, you will never know how much better they would have done with you. By the time we realize this, it will be too late, for they will be grown and gone. Young women naturally want to run – to be a part of the action outside of the home. Home gets boring – the excitement is in the marketplace.

(Young women, honestly, don't you think it is odd when a young woman wants to keep house, and watch babies? Isn't she a little wierd, bovine, or dull?)

WHY DO WE NEED TO BE HOME WITH OUR CHILDREN?

When we brought a child into the world, we started something we will never finish unless they die before their time. A child is only lent to us.

They have it all to learn, and we are to be their favorite teachers because we love them more than anyone else does – or should. We willingly take on their responsibilities. We choose to sit up with them at night and take them to the doctor's when they are ill. We have the awesome chore of shaping their minds and attuning them to God. We are responsible for their thought, actions, ideals and character, and we cannot delegate this to anyone else nor should we want to.

I have seen young Christian women teaching their babies about God before they could talk. I have even seen babies whose first word was "God." What wise mothers!

Do we ask them after their Bible classes what they learned? (One time we asked our small son whom he studied about that Sunday morning. He answered, "Adam McGeve.")

Every day happenings give us many opportunities to point out the goodness or the discipline of God.

"My Mother Loved Me"

There never was a time that my mother didn't love me.
She couldn't wait to see me when I woke up from my sleep.
She hastened to my side every time she heard me weep.
She ran through the house when she heard me at the door –
A smile on her face just to see me back once more.
She trained, tutored, taught me and didn't spare the rod.
She impressed me every day with a desire to please our God.
Her steps are moving slower but one thing I can see.
That through the years I've learned to love her
Just the way that she loved me.

– Lea Fowler

44

OLDER CHILDREN

The influence of home outweighs by *far* any other influence. Home is headquarters. Home is where you talk to them when they get up and when they walk with you and when they retire. *You are their greatest teacher!* I took my children with me from room to room when they were babies and talked to them. When they were old enough, I put them in a walker, and they followed me and talked to me. (They're grown now, but they still follow me from room to room!) When I cooked – as they grew older – they cooked, too and hung out clothes with me and worked with me on whatever tasks had to be done. We worked together, read together, napped together, and prayed together.

You are developing a lifelong relationship, friendship, partnership, and loveship. You are learning to know and to love your child, and they are learning to know and love you.

Dr. Campbell says that "most parents *have a feeling of love* toward their children and that they assume that the child knows it, but often he does not." He says, "that the greatest error today with parents is that they do not convey their great love to the child." He says, "the reason they do not is because they do not know how. So, the children do not feel genuinely, unconditionally loved and accepted. Because of this, everything is on a faulty foundation and discipline, peer relationships, and school perform- ance all suffer. Problems will result."

How can we show them how much we love them when we are not with them? How can we give them ourselves when our *prime time* is given to others? Our children are getting "leftover" parents, and we are raising "leftover" children.

It really takes twenty-one years to bring up a child to be a young adult. I understand that the Jewish people used to say that a man is not a man until he is thirty, and there is a lot of truth in that. They can grow up without our constant care, but they will not be what they *could have been* without careful parenting from a parent who gives them quality *and* quan- tity time.

Peanuts says, "Happiness is hearing your mother's voice in the kitchen when you come home from school."

When they come home from school is such an important time. There is so much to tell and fix and share. By the time parents come in at supper- time, the news is forgotten or put away because of harried parents with too many burdens of their own.

Most of us are familiar with the term "latch-key" children. These are children who come home to an empty house with their own key. Over three million children between the ages of 6 and 13 go home to an empty house. An estimated 50,000 *preschoolers* are home alone.

"A child left to himself will bring his mother to shame" (Proverbs 29:15). Why not a father to shame? Because God knows that a father must work to feed his family, but that chore was not put on the mother. Child raising is often placed solely on the mothers though God teaches the fathers are to become more and more involved. *Someone* has to be with the children, and the punishment of Adam still must be paid daily by the man of the household.

Some women have to work, and God knows and understands that. But often women are working for THINGS. Drugs and liquor are at an all time high as well as abortion, pregnant teenagers and suicides of teenagers. *Where did all the mothers go?*

"The latch-key child goes home and often hides. They hide in a shower or under the bed or in a closet or bathroom. They often turn up the TV at a loud volume and the parents never know because their children don't tell them." One girl said, "Because we don't want to worry her" (exerpts from *People* magazine on "Latch-Key Children.")

It is critical for children and parents to have a close, loving bond and this will seldom be if the children are left to themselves. God pities the widows and the orphans, and how shall we answer when *we* make our children orphans?

I can hear the protests — "I have to work." "We could not live as we do without me working." That might be true, but can we live a little lower and trust God to see that we have enough? Are we giving as we are prospered to God? If we are, God is giving it back pressed down and running over.

Can't we find ways at home to help financially as the worthy woman did? God knows how to supply our needs. I worked part time when my children reached college age and can testify that it costs to work outside of the home. Many times it costs the second car with all its expenses, better clothes, a quicker more expensive way of cooking. (It takes energy, and planning and studying to know how to economize plus the desire to do so.)

The woman, as God knows, does not have the physical stamina to work all day and then come home to do all she would have done if she had been at home. Hurry causes anger, and even children's needs can cause anger. The husband not taking the lead causes fresh daily anger, and the child often goes to bed feeling unloved and unwanted.

God doesn't tell us *why* to stay home and what the results will be when we don't. We know *why* often too late when the harm is done, and the twig is bent, and the die is cast. This is one of the reasons that He instructs the older women to teach the younger women. "Don't let them lose their children," God says. (You know when we lose our children, God usually loses them, too.)

46

Dr. Campbell stresses that our children must feel unconditionally loved. "If we leave the impression with them that we love them *only IF* they do this and that, they will grow up to be incompetent and insecure." After all, if they cannot succeed with us – their parents – how can they expect the world to receive and appreciate them?

"Children *reflect* love; they do not start it." Our love or lack of it shows through them. Psychologists treating troubled children use a doll and watch a child play with the doll. Their actions show how they feel about their parents' love for them. Think about it! How would our children act with a doll to reflect *our* love and attention?

TOUCHING

Somewhere, somehow, someone is going to HAVE to start this touching business. If our foundation in marriage is right, we are showing our love for each other, and the children are seeing it or the lack of it.

I've heard many people say that their families did not touch – and this is why *they* do not touch. *Touching is absolutely imperative!* Hug, touch, look with loving eyes at each other.

Dr. Campbell says that our children should have a love tank. A reservoir of laid up love that will help him in the difficult times. Keep filling his tank up and replenishing it. *You can't love a child too much!* You can spoil him by giving him things that hurt him, but you cannot give too much love. They need to see approval and affection in our eyes constantly. "A child never forgets or forgives a parent who won't look at him. It makes him feel un-loved and worthless" – Campbell.

A boy's first seven years need to be full of touching, cuddling, fondling, hugging, and kissing. (Nursing gives you a head start.) Research shows that girl infants less than 12 months old receive five times as much touching as boys do! *This shows why we have more trouble with boys.* Dr. Campbell also teaches us, "Many people do not like any children and a lot of people find boys around eight unappealing, irritating, and often ob-noxious." We need to examine our own feelings and work on them if we find this reaction within ourselves.

"Girls do not show their emotional needs as much as boys in their first eight years. But they suffer intensely at lack of touching. With the girl, her peak of emotional needs is around eleven years of age. They need it then, and they especially need the attention of their fathers" Campbell.

THE THINGS WE OWE

We owe our children security-physical, spiritual, and emotional. Some day they are going out into the world, and the world owes them nothing. If we have filled our children's "love tank" with what it needs, they can take the impatience of the school teacher, the pain of the bullies, and the competition of their peers. This is one of the reasons that we need to be with them when they come in the door.

FORGIVENESS

Parents need to practice and teach forgiveness. God gives us a new day each day, and we don't have yesterday's strength. Don't hold grudges against your children. Don't hold their inborn temperaments against them. Forgive them for reminding you of your own imperfections or someone else's in the family. *"Don't punish a truly repentant child"* – Campbell.

Teach them to be conscious of their own sins and to fix them with God and others. Teach them to know that the forgiven sin is at the bottom of the sea. Let them see *you* fix your sins and note your comfort because your sin is forgiven.

We used to have a little dog house with five pegs on it and our names written on each of the pegs. When one of us offended another and would not fix it, his name was placed in the dog house. The only way you could get it out was to repent and say, "I'm sorry." It was a healthy way of creating a good conscience. (And our children got to see their parents repenting, too.)

God tells us to raise our children in the Lord. "Children, obey your parents in the Lord for this is right" (Ephesians 6:1).

All sin *must* be repented for or punished. Our sins do find us out. God is not fooled. "Whatever a man sows that shall he reap" (Galatians 6:7). Fix the sin, and then refill the love tank.

HOW ABOUT THE ROD?

"The rod and reproof give wisdom" (Proverbs 29:15). There's not much reproof that you can give a toddler, and there's not much need of a rod for a teenager. If we have been constant and totally involved as parents should be in the training of our children, reproof is about all they need as they grow older. It is only the fool's back that needs the stripes.

The one thing we must never permit with our children is defiance or rebellion. This is an attitude of having to have one's own way. It is a meeting of wills and a determination to win at any cost. These occasions arise with every child because "foolishness is bound in the heart of the child and the rod of correction will drive it far from him" (Proverbs 22:15).

If we have been the loving parents that we should be, the child will hurriedly seek to restore the loving relationship. A rebellious child is at war, and he *has* to know that he is not going to win the war. (Pity the child that *does* win.) There is a principle here – a principle of obedience and authority. "Correct your son, and he will give you comfort; he also will

48

delight your soul" (Proverbs 29:17).

If we are having too many battles, then we need to see what *we* are doing wrong. Maybe we are over strict and unrealistic with our children, and our desires for them are unrealistic, too. We have to continually pray for wisdom. *God knows how to raise children, and we don't!*

A child soon learns if we are being fair or unfair. They soon learn when we really want them to mind and when it is important to us. They continue to test us to see where the boundaries are. Many parents do not know that children *need* boundaries for security.

We are trying to teach *them* how to be good parents. The oldest child is usually a different child. Either we were too strict or too lenient. We gradually change – hopefully for the better. We learn that a fault is not necessarily a permanent part of his character.

Haven't you often heard the question – how can one child turn out badly when all the others did well, and they had the same parents? No, they really didn't have the same parents. We are learning and changing, and we tend to change our methods as we grow older. It is usually conceded that the very young or the very old should not raise children. We tend to be too strict when we are very young and too permissive when we are very old.

After the rod has been applied to the posterior and the tears are flowing, sobs and snuffling are in evidence, then what? "Give them time to cry awhile and think awhile, but stay near to pick up the pieces and refill the love tank" – Campbell. It is a mistake to start loving them immediately. This is confusing to them. They should have been warned what the consequences would be if they disobeyed and then told again during the make up session. They need to be reassured that you still love them though they themselves probably wonder why! "They should always be aware that there is *nothing* they can do that will stop your love but also that love is a part of enforcing the rules" – Campbell.

How many times have you heard people say that the Bible says, "Spare the rod and spoil the child.?" It does *not* say that, rather it says, "He that spareth the rod hateth his own child" (Proverbs 13:24). Some love their children so much that they cannot spank them; others love theirs so much, they can!

When your child is still rebellious after the spanking, you stopped too soon. They will rush to be loved when the chastisement was right. The love tank needs to be refilled, and they know it.

Another point that needs to be brought up about here is – parents are *always* responsible for their children wherever they are. We have all had children visit our homes who apparently belonged to no one. They were allowed to jump on the beds, hit other children, and fall on the floor in hysterics. No one moves. The hostess does not dare; the other mothers don't know what to do, and the child is free to terrorize. (Usually the mother does not want this child to be corrected.) Somehow she feels she is on neutral ground, and the child gets in free. I have even heard parents say after they are struck by their own child. "He feels he has me over a barrel because we are around company." Who gave him that feeling?

It seems unbelievable that you have to tell many parents that they are not to allow themselves or others to be hit by their own children. Some even laugh at it and think it cute. But it won't be that funny when your child is old enough to injure another, even the parents themselves. YOU ARE TO BE IN CONTROL OF YOUR CHILD. If he is *not* your responsibility, whose is he?

Have you ever noticed the emotional stability of such a little tyrant's mother? She is frazzled and harried. She knows the child is out of control, and she feels almost immobilized by the child's forceful behavior. Somehow she lost the upper hand, but God says that not only can she regain control, but she can also have peace again in the home — and in other people's homes. Again, look at Proverbs 29:17: "Correct your son, and he will give you rest; He will also delight your soul."

PRETEACHING

I have found a lot of help in "preteaching." For instance, you might say, "We are going into the Smith's house, and you are not going to jump on the bed, hit others, or throw fits. If you do, I will do this and *then you do that.* Never let your child intimidate you. It isn't right, and he knows it isn't right. He will lose respect for you if you continue in this sort of non-action. You can go into a private room, or car or just go home and do the discipline, but DO IT for everybody's sake. (A well-disciplined child notes the undisciplined with disapproval.)

If you cannot keep your child in control in public or will not, then you need to stay home until you can or will. You may have to hire a babysitter for a while, but in the meantime, you must be learning how to produce a lovely child. God will help you if you'll ask Him. So will older women. (One is not justified to forsake the assembly — Hebrews 10:25).

A tyrant child is an unloved child by others, and how can we let *our* child be an unloved child? The rod, reproof, and love are our answers.

After the confrontation remember there needs to be a lot of love — not indulgence — but love, sharing, laughing, praising when you can. As Dale Carnegie says, "Be hearty in your approbation and lavish in your praise." Every human needs it.

"It is by his deeds that a lad distinguishes himself if his conduct is pure and right" (Proverbs 20:11?.

It is difficult to endure sound teaching — *especially to mothers about their children.* We are emotional tigers about our children.

Hebrews 12:9-10 states, "Furthermore, we had earthly fathers to discipline us, and we respected them . . . for they disciplined us for a short time *as seemed best to them.*" And we, as their children, benefited or suffered or both. This causes us to be on the defensive and to answer quickly when reprimanded — "You raise yours your way, and I'll raise mine my way."

What is God after with us? What is He trying to produce in us, His children? Holiness, righteous living, happiness here and eternal life with Him. So, He continues to discipline us daily. " And reproofs for discipline are the way of life" (Proverbs 6:23b).

We discipline our children for "a short time." God knows just how short it is before they are gone. God knows if we aren't rightly raising our children, then we are wrongly raising them. If wrong, they will never be holy, righteous, happy here or with Him in eternity. He tries to get our attention, and one way is through older Christian women.

Can we love our children enough to lovingly listen to you, older woman? Holy Father?

THOUGHT QUESTIONS

1. Are Christian women often influenced by the examples of worldly women?

2. Is it a temptation to leave our responsibilites?

3. What if our "responsibilities" were taken away from us?

Chapter 5
TO SHOW EXTRA LOVE
TO THEIR TEENAGERS
(OR IS THERE LIFE AFTER TEENAGERS?)

Al Capp, the cartoonist, says to lock them up until they are 21! Some parents say, "I have never had trouble with my teenagers." But, the majority say, "Help!"

As I began to write this chapter, the thought came to me that you raise your teenagers with the same recipes you used with the younger ones. Let's review some of those worthy ways:

1. The father takes full responsibility for his family, leading in love.

2. The mother and children in the same room talking to each other.

3. Show the child you love it unconditionally.

4. Continue to daily replenish his love tank.

5. Touch, touch, touch.

6. The parents practice and teach forgiveness.

7. Use rod and reproof – much less rod and much more reproof. Authority is maintained.

8. Be responsible for your child wherever he is and whomever he's with.

9. Worship with your child; sit together as a family; pray together often. Talk on the way home about what was preached and taught. End each day with prayer for that

day to end right. Start each day with a prayer for that day.

— Some suggestions by Campbell)

The talking continues day and night. Different words are used, but the teachers are the same. As a parent you realize that these are the dangerous years. They are old enough to drive, date, choose the wrong companions, and run away from home. That's scary!

In one night they can be killed in a wreck, lose their virginity, hold up a liquor store with a bad bunch, or be picked up on a lonely road by a sex offender.

"The time to counsel a young person is before he falls in love. The time to show the perils of riches is before he gets rich. The time to teach obedience is in the playpen instead of the State Pen" — Anonymous.

Their energy is doubling while ours is halving. They have all the answers, and we have all the problems. They are only ready to confide and ask for advice after midnight when you can't keep your eyes open. He wants advice after a date. Her hair must be rolled, heated, blown or whatever just before dawn. They are so beautiful, so talented, and so impossible!

Touch, touch, touch, and give them lots of loving eye contact. Our son wiggled and demanded to be put down from five months old until he was a senior in high school. He liked eye contact and approval but seemed to draw back from physical touching. When he was in high school, I was telling this in front of him to a friend. After the friend left, he said, "I don't know why you feel that way. I like to be touched!"

"From now on," I said, "you *will* be touched — if I have to hold you down." (Think of all those years that I thought I was pleasing him by *not* touching him. What a waste for him and me.)

Get up and take them where they need to be. Don't let them miss a teenage rally. It is *your* responsibility to see that your child attends these things and Christian camp and WHATEVER is good for them. Some day you can rest when they are grown and gone and sad to say, that will not be long. Don't wait for the school or the church or other parents to see or provide what your child needs. *That's a cop-out.*

The usual complaint a teenager has about his parents is that they do not understand him. Really, what they are saying is, "They do not listen to me." Not only are we to talk to them but we are to listen to them. They have a lot to say, and too often we are not listening. And, they know it.

LET THEM BE THEMSELVES

While I was writing this chapter, I questioned several teenagers about their feelings. What would they do differently in raising their own children than the way they are being raised?

One girl said, "I would not compare one child with another. I would accept each child for himself."

Let's talk about that. We must realize again that each person is born with his or her natural temperament that cannot be altered much. "The race is not to the swift," God says, but we want our children to be "swift" students and bring home good grades. Some of them *cannot,* and we *must not* demand the impossible!

No matter how many children we have, each one is different. They are each unique. They are not like each other or can they be.

We *must* let them be themselves. This is sometimes a hard lesson for us parents to learn and *accept.* (I am reminded of my youngest daughter whose theme song was "I Gotta Be Me.")

Each has a special God-given place in this world, and we must encourage them to find their comfortable and useful niche in the kingdom. They need to be accepted for themselves!

"Let Me Be Me!"

Let me be me − I'm not her, you see.
She's fancy and girlie, likes buttons and bows.
I like tailored things and simply made clothes.
She's content with quantity and multiple choice.
The dress that's classy and chic gets my choice.
She gets sleepy at nine and goes right to bed.
Somehow it's around twelve before I lay down my head.
She gives in easily, dissolves into tears
While I'm up on my soap box defending my fears.
She crawls on your lap − heaven's above!
Here we're alike − "Move over, my love."

− Lea Fowler

TEACH BY SHARING NOT ASSIGNING

We learn more by *seeing* than by being told what to do. For years I tried successfully to make a good pie crust. The instructions said, "Add as much water as needed." By the time I did this, the crust needed to be kneaded!

Then, I watched a good cook make a pie crust. I found out how much water *was* needed. I took her recipe, followed her example, and now mine are as good as hers. God says to "train up a child." Train means to do it over and over until we have learned the act or art.

Teach, train and brag. We all like to please and be found approvable.

A lady said the other day, "Unless a child is useful, he feels useless." I used to apply good works to the schedule of the day when the children became bored and wanted to fight. "Just put all that energy to doing some things that need to be done." *You* may have to do it with them, but everyone is happier in the end – not mentioning the tasks that were accomplished. Besides, they will never forget the fun of working together, having you to themselves, and accomplishing a great deal. (And they usually wind up repeating this work principle with their own children someday.) I did.

I still delight in memories of my father who had to be our father and mother. About once a year he decided it was time to wash woodwork. (He might have been harnessing our energy from mischief to good works.) So, he provided each of the three of us with a pan of warm soapy water and a rag. Then, he told us where we were to work and set his watch for thirty minutes and said, "Go, see what you can do in that length of time. Remember you only get thirty mintues!" We worked feverishly and then all inspected the marvelous job we had done. All of us worked, and all of us gloried in clean woodwork. Smart Daddy. Precious memories.

"Our Sons"

For the time when a boy is in danger of going a little bit wild,
Is when he's too young to be married, too old to be known as a child.
A bird of the wild grass thicket, just out of the parent tree flown.
Too large to keep in the old nest, too small to have one of his own.
When desolate 'mid his companions, his soul is a stake to be won.
'Tis then that the devil stands ready to get a good place to catch on.

– Anonymous

They are at their peak sexually at seventeen. Their bodies remind them of sexual needs. Their school companions brag about their conquests. Curiosity, need, and example are powerful temptations to experiment, to sin.

Sports are good for boys, for they use up a lot of energy. Jobs are good for the same reason. God says, "It is good for a man that he should bear the yoke in his youth" (Lamentations 3:27). Why? Well, for one reason, it keeps him busy and out of trouble. It is good for him to help the family financially and to feel responsible for some of his own needs. It makes him more serious and less frivolous. It makes his bed look good at night and takes away the yearning to be out on the town. It fights boredom. It sobers him up.

Boys used to live on the farm. Many got up each morning at four A.M.

and started the many chores. After chores and breakfast, many of them had to walk to school. After school they walked home and started the chores again.

Looking back, we feel sorry for them and for such a hard schedule. However, wisdom says that it was good for them. It helped them the rest of their lives to not fear work and to realize what a man's life was all about. An easy life often leads to an easy divorce and grandma raising the children.

Get to know their friends – all of their friends – boys and girls. Have them as part of the Open House life. Let them confide in you. Respect them and learn to love them, too.

Boys need their fathers so much when they are teenagers. They need a male image to admire. Many psychologists believe that a boy raised without a man's lead often tends to homosexuality. *Mothers can never be fathers no matter how hard they try.* They can only be mothers. City boys need to be out of the house and with their fathers hunting and fishing and golfing or whatever. I have heard it said, "If you hunt *with* your boy, you won't have to hunt *for* him."

And a boy always needs a mother. He needs to be with a woman and learn from her about the way women think. Boys need to be tender with the weaker sex – their mothers and their sisters. Many men do not like women. Many men fear women. How can we teach our boys to feel about womankind as God would have them feel?

"Men who do not give into their softer feelings and cultivate them wind up hard on women in time" – Theodore Rubin.

When the mother has to be the stern disciplinarian because there is no father, or if the father is gone all of the time, of if the father is home but abdicates his responsibilites, it sets up the danger of the boy becoming a man who dislikes women. A boy needs to be disciplined by a man even though it often causes temporary rebellion. (In time most men love their fathers for the past discipline and even brag about how hard their Dads were on them.)

It is not good for the teenage boy to exult because he is superior to his mother in strength and brawn. This tends to provoke cruelty in him. The father should be the buffer and should demand obedience and respect for the mother. This is a demonstration for the son's future dealings with his own wife and daughters.

There is an alarming increase in abusive husbands, or wife beaters. These men come from every level of education and financial standard. Why are so many men cruel to their wives? Is this fact just now coming out from under cover or has something happened lately to the American homes? I think it is the latter.

These men were not taught as boys to love and respect their mothers and sisters. As boys, they often did not really know their mothers. They were not raised with the daily love contact and discipline that should have been there. Some of them were those fearful little boys hiding in the closets and under the bed while they were alone.

Many of them did not know they were loved because the parents did not know how to show them. How could it all have been changed? *God's wisdom — obedience to God's way.* "It is not in man that walketh to direct his own steps" (Jeremiah 10:23).

HOW WE LOVE OUR SONS!

Oh, how we love our sons! How we identify with David at the death of his handsome Absalom. "And thus he said as he walked, 'O my son Absalom, my son, my son, Absalom! Would I had died instead of you. O Absalom my son, my son" (2 Samuel 19:33b). And this son died trying to kill his father. I don't know about you, but I can't read this without tears.

Our sons, our heritage, our name bearers, our heart carrier — how many times would we have put them under our wings, but they would not!

This brings to my mind a well written poem that touches my heart.

"Forgive"

O child, our love for you was so fierce and tender!
Use the mistakes our very ardor made
As vaults to planes which otherwise would be unknown.
Knowing an accounting shall be given for your own answer to our faults,
And in such using, forgive, forgive!

— Anonymous

SUICIDE—THE GREATEST HEARTBREAK OF ALL

Each year five thousand young people take their own lives. This is three times the figure of thirty years ago. Most of these are young males. (The adult figures stay about the same.)

What has caused these terrible statistics? *Think about it.* You can probably give some motives without deep meditation. The lack of family ties is number one: "broken homes, divorce, and the slow alienation of the family from each other."

We've seen the TV ad, "Do You Know Where Your Children Are?" There is another — "Do You Know Where Your Parents Are?"

How long would we expect a thriving business to live if those in authority abdicated? How long would *any* sort of an institution last without proper authority and wise supervision? Not long.

But homes are supposed to produce stable wonderful children with the adults habitually absent. Who said so? Not God.

DRUGS AND ALCOHOL

The world has become addicted! It is international. It's not just America. Because of the wealth here, the pushers concentrate on America.

It takes time for parents to recognize and realize that their children are users. Many times it is too late by the time that this fact is established. Then there is a slow death of suicide with parents dying, too – of a broken heart.

LACK OF EMOTIONAL SUPPORT

A quote from *Ladies Home Journal* on this problem says, "There's a lack of involvement with parents, who have their own jobs and interests. So the children often feel that yes, they have it nice, but who around them really gives a "hoot"?

Teenagers need to have been trained to withstand disappointments, to finish their assigned jobs, and to know that whatever the difficult situation, it will pass.

In other words, they need the daily teaching of God's word for comfort and for discipline.

THE REALITY OF DEATH

There are few homes of today like the Waltons on TV. Homes with grandma and grandpa who are involved with the daily raising of the children are rare indeed.

Our young people are unfamilar with death. They see it in movies, but they have witnessed few, if any, deaths of their family members – even their grandparents.

I think we should familiarize our children with death. Take them to a funeral home. Show them death is final and a part of life. (Be sure and make this first introduction at the death of an acquaintance, or a friend. If their first experience is the death of a close relative or a close friend, they will not understand the concept you are trying to convey to them. This kind of death is very heart-wrenching for them.)

Most suicidal young people die not really wanting to die. They just want to escape the temporary pain they are suffering. They don't want to be lonely. They don't know things can get better. They cannot see that there is light at the end of the tunnel.

THE ANSWER

The greatest answer is – be there!! Be conscious if there are too many moods and depressions. Don't let them stay behind closed doors.

Show them how *much* you love them! "Most important is that they be encouraged to talk about their problems with parents or other sympathetic adults . . . If you are picking up a signal, it's up to you to say something in a caring, loving way. This kid needs help" – Dr. Klagsbrien.

"Suicidal kids just want to know someone cares" – George Cohen.

(The past 2 pages have included excerpts from "The Riddle of Teenage Suicide" by Michael J. Weiss from *Ladies Home Journal,* June, 1984.)

"Roadside Reflections"

If this is not a place
where tears
are understood –
where do I go to cry?

If this is not a place
where my spirits
can take wing –
where do I go to fly?

If this is not a place
where my questions
can be asked –
where do I go to seek?

If this is not a place
where my feelings
can be heard –
where do I go to speak?

If this is not a place
where you'll accept
me as I am –
where do I go to be?

If this is not a place
where I can try, and
learn and grow –
where do I go to be me?

– Anonymous

OUR DAUGHTERS

There is such a different feeling for your sons than your daughters. Boys are to be taken seriously and readied for the presidency, and girls are to be squeezed and hugged and dressed up as dolls. Remember Dr. Campbell saying that the girl infants receive five times as much touching as the boy infants during the first twelve months of life?

That is a lot of difference, *too much difference*. It is easy for the mother to understand the daughter because she used to be a little girl. Her parents probably indulged her and still do.

Remembering is *important* in being a good mother. Remember when you wanted your first high heels *and* your Easter basket on the same day? Remember when you liked any boy that liked you except for ---. (There was always an exception.)

Girls giggle and stay up late, try on cosmetics and consider dyeing their hair some awful color. They are noisy and dramatic. They suffer wholeheartedly and are usually close to tears. And when they cry because their nose is too large or they think themselves too fat or their feet too big or whatever, they are inconsolable. (Anorexia is almost epidemic.)

The new Brooke Shields trend has little girls looking as if they are twenty-five. They look like they are dressed in Mama's clothes. The world demands of them maturity, and they cannot deliver. There are many twelve year old prostitutes and will probably be many more. How sad.

But, if you have continued your good raising, have filled the love tank daily, continued eye contact and touch, close family ties, prayed and stayed together, grew together — *you have produced your best girlfriends for l i f e !*

There is nothing that you cannot discuss, though they may ask questions you have never heard discussed and are not sure how to answer. And you don't want to know. But you do not act shocked, and you say, "Let me think about it." Then, you hunt for a Bible answer *and pray.*

THE DAILY APPOINTMENT

I can't stress enough how important it is for the family to be together for an unhurried meal once a day. *This is a tie that must not be broken or neglected!* This should be the time that the family has anticipated all day. This is the time to laugh together, to review the day's happenings, and to share family thoughts. Mama has prepared a lovely meal. Dad has rested some and is ready to eat and enjoy his family. (Visiting youngsters may catch their only glimpse of what a family should be.)

Courtesy is taught, and good manners are stressed at the dinner table. I read an article once when drugs were just taking hold of America. People had made a survey of school children in relation to possible future drug users. They had noticed that two things in a child's life in grade school help to prophesy future drug users. One was the parents who popped a lot of pills themselves and the *other was the children who did not eat meals with the parents.*

Eating together is prime time, quality time, socializing time, getting to know each other time. Mothers, this will be up to you to provide these daily experiences and to stress their importance. Fathers, you, too!

CLOTHES

Clothes are very important to teenage girls. They *should* look nice. Good clothes give a feeling of self worth. They help in difficult times to respect oneself. Shopping together should be quality fun time for a mother and daughter. This is a time for a lot of eye contact and touching and approval. This is shopping with your best girl friend. It is also a time for a modesty lesson and a teaching of selecting clothes that will last, instead of the current fad.

DADS

Dads are especially appreciated by teenage girls. Most girls tend to marry a man a lot like their fathers – especially if they have had a good relationship with them. It is good for you to encourage them to have time alone together, to eat out, etc. A time for father-daughter talks. A father misses so much if he doesn't get to know his daughters, and I don't believe he will know them accidentally.

THE WHITE DRESS

Satan says, "Everybody's doing it. Virgins are passe. Men expect women of today to be knowledgeable about sex. It is desirable to be experienced." This is the devil's lie, and he is the father of all lies.

God says, "Flee fornication" (1 Corinthians 6:18). He uses the term fornication rather than adultery, for it is the broader term that covers all sexual uncleanness.

Joseph of old, the boy with the beautiful colored coat made by his father, must have had good parents. When he was rejected by his brothers and sold into slavery, his master's wife said, "Lie with me." He answered, "How then could I do this great evil and sin against God?" (Genesis 39:9b).

Do we raise our children with the repeated teaching that sex outside of marriage is a a great evil? And do we even more importantly teach them that unlawful sex is a sin against God?

God says, "Run for your life." Solomon teaches his young son about the adulterous woman. "To deliver you from the strange woman, from the adulteress who flatters with her words; that leaves the companion of her youth and forgets the covenant of her God; for her house sinks down to death and her tracks lead to the dead; none who go to her return again, nor do they reach the paths of life" (Proverbs 2:16-19).

Warn them to flee from the parked car, or the empty bedroom at home, or the shoddy motel.

God said – run – and Joseph literally ran with her holding onto his coat. He ran out of his coat. Didn't he know about the double standard that says it is all right for the boy but not for the girl?

Have you ever given any thought to Jacob and Rachel? There they lived in the same house, grown, engaged for seven years and stayed pure. Of course, in those days chaperoning was diligently enforced. Many countries still practice this today, and there are not the pregnancies and abortions in those countries that we have.

Many future marriages are ruined by the result of furtive affairs. Guilt, poorly learned sexual practices continue through life, and there is the unfortunate comparisons of sexual partners. I find it rather amusing to read psychologists of the world state that the best marriages are formed by two people who are virgins. God knew that all along.

But many of the teenagers have to taste it all before it's time. And they still want the white dress, the church wedding, the minister's words (instead of the justice of the peace), the ceremony, and the final blessing of the church. "I want it all even though I broke the rules as well as my parents' hearts."

I know of a case where two strong Christian young people married. The girl wore her white gown, and he added a white vest to his attire, for he said, "We both worked at deserving this right – the right to white."

I don't believe I have ever heard of a Christian girl rejoice at losing her virginity outside of marriage. As a matter of fact, I have never heard of the Christian boy rejoicing at such a thing. But I have had many tell me of their sorrow because they didn't wait.

Happiness is found in keeping the commandments from our youth up. Remember when Jesus met the rich young ruler? He loved him at sight because He knew that this was an unusual young man.

"What shall I do to inherit eternal life?" This was the question the young man asked. Jesus answered, "You know the commandments," and He went on to name them.

"And he said to Him, 'Teacher, I have kept all these from my youth up.' "

"And looking at him, Jesus felt a love for him" (Mark 10:17-22).

Why did Jesus feel a love for him? Because he was young, or rich, or a ruler? No, but because he was pure and an obedient youth. Do we teach our young to be pure and pleasing so that they will please their Master? Joseph's parents did. Jacob's parents, also.

God says not only flee, but He gives the reason why. "Every other sin that a man commits is outside the body, but the immoral man sins against his own body" (1 Corinthians 6:18).

What does this scripture mean? It could mean this: we cannot remember every lie we have told, recall every bad word said or every impure thought that we have entertained. But surely most people can remember the name of the person we have had unlawful sex with! It is a big act – the two becoming one flesh. It is the most personal, physical relationship possible. It takes something created by God for a beautiful marriage experience and turns it into a shameful, shoddy, furtive, animal deed.

Parents are taught to raise their children "in the Lord." We greatly fail them when we do not stress moral purity. Do we continue to remind them that their sins will find them out and that whatever they sow they will reap?

PAYDAY IS COMING

Do we teach our children and teenagers not to be ignorant of Satan's devices? Do we assure them that because they are Christians they will be tempted *more* sorely than their non-Christian friends? And they will be tempted even more – especially if their fathers are leaders in the church?

Legion is the number of fallen children of faithful Christians. The heart-break is unbelievable of the parents, the children themselves, and of the church, the body of Christ.

Satan laughs as the parents try to pick up the pieces. Could an older woman have helped *this not to happen?* Could she have thrown up the "No Trespassing" and "Danger" signs to the parents? Could she have said, "Mothers, fathers, do you know where your children are? Do you know if they are virgins? Do you dare talk to them about the dangers of unlawful touching? Do you demand sexual purity? Do you rely on the school or the church *to do your job?* Do your children dare to mention the word "sex" to you and ask all the questions that they hear at school? Is there *anything* that you cannot discuss with them freely? Are you going to force them to learn from their peers and learn it wrong?"

God says, "Awake thou that sleepest" (Ephesians 5:14). Mothers – wake up! Too often the mothers are gone from the home, and the teenagers are using the beds for "nesting."

A *teenager* left to himself will bring his mother to shame, too. If they are being left in the teenage years without the daily, hourly, needed instructions and love, how can a parent catch up? How can the gaps of parental absences and neglected instructions be filled?

REPAIRING THE BREACH

How do we go about righting our lives with our teenage daughters (and sons) if we have just done it all wrong? How do we make a friend of a potential enemy who turns away?

Prayer, wisdom, and communication. Try sitting down and leveling with them. Tell them what is in your heart. Ask for another chance. Ask them to help you to become the mother you want to be and that they want you to be. *Do a lot of listening, unshocked listening.* Young people are usually pretty fair and reasonable when they are approached with honesty and courage. *We've got to try* no matter our age or theirs. God may lead you to heights you thought impossible.

Girls are vulnerable. They can be so easily crushed. They are like a lovely bud who can become a beautiful flower, or they can freeze and die. We can, by our ignorance or stubbornness, forever damage a relationship. Love is a gift; it can never be forced.

Dear Father,

Help us to live in such a way with our children that when they are grown, they will love us more as the years go by. Help them to appreciate our love and care for them. Help them as they raise their children and see all the difficulties and problems, that they will better understand our concerns. May the years wipe away the bad memories and bring in their place, peace and love and the renewing desire to be a FAMILY.

In the Son's name, Amen

IN CONCLUSION

Surely there will be older parents who will read this and say, "Oh, that we could do it all over again, knowing what we do now!" The kids are grown and gone. Some are faithful Christians raising good children: some have fallen away.

You must forgive yourselves, for God has forgiven you, if you've repented. We tend to remember only the bad memories, the negatives, the words we wish we had not said and we forget all the good.

We need to realize that somewhere along the way those young children became old enough to choose right from wrong. *In time we are all responsible for our own sins.*

The mental institutions are filled with guilt-ridden people. I have heard it said by those in the know that over eighty percent of the people are there because of guilt. *This is not God's plan for you!* Don't join those unfortunate people. God isn't through with us or our children yet. He doesn't give His final judgment until our last page on earth is written.

"Confess your faults one to another and be healed" (James 5:16).

"Blaming Godly Parents for Ungodly Behavior"

A young person decides to quit the church and launch out into the world of sin and shame. When approached by some interested person he says, "I have had religion rammed down my throat all my life." Thus his poor old parents, whose hearts are already breaking for him, are made to take the blame for what he is. How inhuman and cruel can one be?

I had food "rammed down my throat" all my life, and I still love to eat. I was made to comb my hair and take a bath all my life, and I still comb my hair and bathe. My mother tried in an uneducated sort of way to teach me right from wrong, and though I have done many things wrong, it never occurred to me to blame my mother for any misbehavior on my part.

My wife and I never rammed religion down our children's throats," unless that is what you call trying to bring them up in the nurture and admonition of the Lord." I could name five young people right now who have thus accused their parents. These young people ought to go to their parents, get on their knees before them and beg for their forgiveness for such base ingratitude and go with them before God and ask His forgiveness.

Young people, if you must be ungodly, don't blame godly parents for your ungodliness. All they ever wanted for you was that you live right. Be a man or women, and face your mistakes. You will give an account at the Judgment.

— Selected

THOUGHT QUESTIONS

1. Name some identical characteristics needed in raising children and teenagers.

2. What are some symptoms of a possibily suicidal teenager?

3. Why do teenagers feel their parents do not understand them?

Chapter 6
TO BE SENSIBLE

"How long will you love being simple?" Or, "How long, O naive ones, will you love simplicity? And scoffers delight themselves in scoffing, and fools hate knowledge?" (Proverbs 1:22).

When are we going to grow up and learn that naivete is child-likeness, and maturity is to be desired? We can't help being young, but with God's daily wisdom, we can leave immaturity and exchange it for happiness and reality. In time.

"We are no longer to be children, tossed here and there by waves, and carried about by every wind of doctrine, by the trickery of men, by craftiness in deceitful scheming" (Ephesians 4:14). We are not to be kids any longer, for if we are, we will be quickly deceived. Satan's favorite tool is deceit. Eve was deceived; she was naive; she was fooled. We don't have an example of her being fooled the second time. Her price of naivete was too great and long lasting. The gates of Eden were forever closed.

It takes time and practice to learn what God says about everything. We can in a good conscience do many things as a new Christian that, in time, we have to put away. "For though by this time you ought to be teachers, you have need again for someone to teach you the elementary principles of the oracles of God, and you have come to need milk and not solid food . . . But solid food is for the mature, who because of practice have their senses trained to discern good and evil" (Hebrews 5:12,14).

These people had gone backwards. They had once been teachers, but now they needed the ABC's again. We, too, are growing, or we are slipping back. We use it or lose it. And if we are not daily in the Word and praying for wisdom in our lives, then we are regressing instead of progressing. It is only by practice that we can train our senses to know what is good and what is evil in the sight of God.

The next verse in Ephesians 4:25 says, "But speaking the truth in love, we are to grow up in all aspects into Him, who is the head, even Christ." We are to grow up and no longer *want* to be a child.

Why would we want to be a child? Because it is hard to be an adult. The buck stops with you instead of the indulgence you once felt. I remember when I went to college. What a shock! My teachers before had always wanted me to pass and encouraged me. To fail would have been just about as hard on them as on me!

I went to a state school during the depression. There were seven male students to every female. The teachers did not want any *children*: rather, they insisted that you be an adult. They called you by "Miss" and "Mr." They assured you that they graded on the curve which means that there would be some who would fail no matter what the grades. They encouraged you to quit if you were not serious about learning. You could attend class or not, keep notes or not, fail or pass. It meant nothing to them whatever your choice. (You really got the message that they hoped you chose to fail so they could be rid of you and would deal only then with the committed.)

You know, if you think about it, God gives this same sort of logic when he says, "I know your deeds, that you are neither cold nor hot; I would that you were cold or hot. So because you are lukewarm, and neither hot nor cold, I will spit you out of my mouth" (Revelation 3:15,16). Which is another way of saying, "Grow up or else!"

It takes us a long time to realize that Christianity is a life-and-death situation. It takes longer to believe that we are not capable of directing our own lives. It takes even more time to realize that we're "by nature children of wrath" and that if we continue to drift, we are going over the falls!

It is "natural" to be lost. It is natural to be selfish. It is natural to be lazy. It is natural to be naive, especially if you are a woman.

It is unnatural to be a worthy woman or a worthy man.

SENSIBLE ABOUT TIME

"Plan your day or lose it." *Do not be ruled by the urgent!* I am convinced that one of the hardest daily tasks that we have is conscientiously getting our priorities straight. God knows what this day should hold and will hold.

Emergencies arise when the urgent *must* be served. But usually a day can be planned and your objectives carried out. We need to assign ourselves three good-sized tasks for the day. Reasonable tasks. *Then do them.*

"Time is like a weaver's shuttle." We think the babies will stay babies, but they don't and before we know it, they are being married. You have heard the old saying that "the road to hell is paved with good intentions."

We mean to get around to training our children, keeping our romance alive, nurturing our children in the way of the Lord, and we sit in shock as they parade in their cap and gown.

Procrastination is a deadly vice. To put off until tomorrow what needs to be done today is slow suicide. "Lord, make me to know my end, and what is the extent of my days, let me know how transient I am. Behold, Thou hast made my days as handbreadths, and my life time as nothing in thy sight. Surely, every man at his best is a mere breath. Surely every man walks about as a phantom" (Psalm 39:4-6a).

Immaturity says, "You have a life time." Maturity says, "Life is short, and you are living now." God says, "I may come today."

> This is the beginning of a new day. God has given me this day to use as I will. I can waste it or grow in its light and be of service to others. But what I do with this day is important because I have exchanged a day of my life for it. When tomorrow comes, today will be gone forever. I hope I will not regret the price I paid for it.
>
> – Anonymous

We may think we have more time than money. We may have more money. "Redeem the time" (Ephesians 5:16). Buy it. Use it. There are jobs today that must be done or prices to pay for them left undone.

SENSIBLE ABOUT MONEY

Many of us are uncomfortable with the verse that says, "A fool and his money are soon parted." Nor do we cherish the old saying that "money burns a hole in our pocket." Yet, we would all agree that mature people should be wiser spenders than the immature.

God loves to say Yes. He wants us to have our heart's desires in time – in His time. He tells us how much better He can give gifts than we can to our children. When we look back at the patriarchs of the Old Testament, we find them to be wealthy men, very wealthy men.

The book of Job was written to show us that a good man can have bad things happen to him, and he can lose his wealth and health. It was a belief at that time that good health and wealth were given only to good men and that bad things happened only to bad people. It is still generally so that blessings come with a consecrated life. (We must always remember the end of the Lord. Job was saved and his fortunes restored – even doubled.)

God loves to give, for He is the great giver. God is love, and love gives and gives. But God has a plan for His giving, and we need to find and execute His plan. His will is for us to give as we are prospered, and then He will give it back pressed down and running over (1 Corinthians 16:2, 2 Corinthians 9:7, Luke 6:38). This has always been a principle of God's law – both to the Jew and to the Christian.

He throws out the challenge under the old law: "Bring the whole tithe into the storehouse, so that there may be food in My house, and test me now in this," says the Lord of hosts, "if I will not open for you the windows of heaven, and pour out for you a blessing until there is no more need" (Malachi 3:10).

God says, "You give first, and then I'll give back." *That takes faith. I'll pour our generously,*" says the Lord. (When Christians come to me with financial problems, I always ask first, "How is your giving?" Usually the answer is right there.)

Sometimes it is not in the giving but in the using. *We by nature want too much too soon.* It would not be good for us to get things too soon because the human being is never satisfied.

"He who loves money will not be satisfied with money, nor he who loves abundance with its income. This too is vanity" (Ecclesiastes 5:10). "You cannot serve God and money," the New Testament teaches in Luke 16:13.

God wants to gradually take us into a blessed world *as we become more blessed people.* We upset His plan when both the parents have to be busy making money, and the children suffer for it. Maturity sees this, but naivete and selfishness want it all NOW. The price is too steep!

SENSIBLE ABOUT GOOD COMPANIONS

"Birds of a feather flock together." We tend to choose for friends those we like rather than those we would be like. Our criteria for their being a part of our lives is: do they make me laugh? Do we have about the same finances? Do we like the same people? Are our husbands pleased with their husbands? Are we compatible? (Note that we haven't mentioned spirituality!) Do they make us better people when we are together? Are they really striving to please God? Do they take seriously the proper raising of their children? Do I admire them for their goodness?

"Do not be deceived: 'Bad company corrupts good morals' " (1 Corinthians 15:33). Many times we have to gradually change our close friends. Some friends are too expensive – spiritually speaking. They bring out the worst in us not the best. We tend to be lax where they are lax. They tempt us to worldliness. We cannot afford them.

A sweet Christian lady gave us this saying once at a Ladies' Day, and I treasure it. "A rule to govern my life: Anything that dims my vision of Christ or takes away my taste for Bible study or cramps my prayer life or makes Christian work difficult is wrong for me. I must, as a Christian, turn away from it."

The book of Proverbs has so much to say about the danger of bad companions and how this relationship can even cause death. How many sweet young people got in the wrong crowd and didn't live long enough to be conscious of the danger? Legions. Immaturity doesn't recognize the danger of the wrong associations. They feel that they are in control when they are not.

No human body can allow drugs, alcohol, promiscuous sex, abuse of the body, abuse of the mind to have its control without paying the piper. Maturity knows that payday is coming, but the grasshopper continues to exult in the warmth of summer.

We need to cultivate, to seek out, the best there are in the church where we meet. God tells us to appreciate our elders. He puts the responsibility on us to seek them out and esteem them. 1 Thessalonians 5:12,13 says, "But we request of you, brethren, that you appreciate those who diligently labor among you, and have charge over you in the Lord and give you instructions, and that you esteem them very highly in love because of their work. Live in peace with one another."

God tells us to call the most righteous for prayer when we have sick ones, for God is nearer to the most righteous.

> *Is anyone among you sick? Let him call for the elders of the church, and let them pray over him, anointing him with oil in the name of the Lord; and the prayer offered in faith will restore the one who is sick, and the Lord will raise him up, and if he has committed sins, they will be forgiven him. Therefore, confess your sins to one another, and pray for one another, so that you may be healed. The effective prayer of a righteous man can accomplish much.*
>
> *— James 5:14,16*

If you are a younger woman, seek out the godly older women for advice. Become dear friends. Get involved in their lives for your own good. If you are an older godly woman, keep your latch string off and your telephone ready for their ring. You may help to save a soul, a family.

Watch your TV companions. You will learn to emulate the wicked woman if you are not careful. Watch your reading companions. There are both kinds. There are some new books you have to burn and some programs that you must turn off.

A WINNER OF SOULS

"He that winneth souls is wise" (Proverbs 11:20). There are those who feel no compulsion to win souls. They excuse themselves because they have young children, or they don't know enough to try to teach others, or God doesn't expect them to win souls but to just please their husbands. Then there is the other extreme. "I am commanded to win souls, so I am justified to leave my children, neglect my house, be so busy serving God that I am released from my home commitments."

Either extreme is wrong. The happy medium is God *does* expect a woman to put her family and home first. Neglected children and dirty houses are abhorrent to God as well as to the world. These actions cause God to be blasphemed rather than glorified. I heard a godly man say, "When a woman is changing her baby's diaper, she is doing the work of the Lord." That's true.

But am I excluded from personal work until my children are grown? Certainly not. Jesus set the example that we must be about our Father's business. There are times we can have our Bible study no matter what the ages of the children. There are occasions when we can attend a Ladies Day, gospel meetings, ladies' classes, etc. There are times we can sit beside a friend and open our Bibles together, and we can teach a person how to become a Christian. But these will have to be planned times.

In a locality where I used to live, the ladies met one day a week and went out to do personal work. Some of the older ladies babysat for the younger ones. This gave the young mothers a chance to be out and away from their responsibilities for awhile. They went to see other young mothers and talked with them and taught them.

If you have children who are very young but are on a workable schedule where you can put them to bed early, then you can have a couple in for social times and for Bible studies. We used to spend many hours like this with other young couples. This way we didn't have to pay a sitter, and we were close to the children if we were needed.

"First a friend and then a brother" is the saying we have written on our church stationery. *It is the most successful way to teach.* People have to know you before they will let you teach them. Eating together is such a good way for the beginning of personal work. We have had more success with that approach than any other in the mission fields of New England, and I believe that it will work everywhere. "Becoming all things to all men" starts with getting to know them.

These "couple" nights are also important to your marriage. The pulling together in the yoke of marriage takes a lot of practice. It gives much happiness and contentment at the end of the evening to know that you were allowed to do something for Him. It makes your life happier and your love grow for your spouse who has the same ideals.

BECOMING A REALIST

God wants us to leave naivete and become adults, and this means becoming realists. Jesus *knew* what was in the heart of man. Do we expect every Christian to act like one? Do we unrealistically demand perfection of every or any older Christian?

Dale Carnegie tells us in his book *How to Win Friends and Influence People* that though we expect people to act unemotionally and wisely, we are *all* unpredictable. We are all the product of our natural born temperaments, environments, schools, churches, books we've read, shows we've seen, etc., etc., etc.

Who says what's normal and to be expected? God takes us where He finds us and tries to bring us with our individual potentialities to where He wants us. He wants us to die to self and become like Him. Too often we are offended if we feel another is not as serious as we are about this Christian life. We quickly become judgmental and mark that person off. But, God is a realist. He knows the heart, thoughts, the background and potential, an He judges impartially. We have to learn to do the same.

God commands us to love even if the other does not love us. We have only to answer for ourselves and should pray for them when they cannot love us. (Yet strive to be lovable.)

Pure religion is hard to come by. It means loving the unlovely. It means helping the ones we would rather not help. It means foot-washing. It means work. We excuse ourselves and others who draw back from service, but that is immaturity. Really, it's just sin.

James 2 tells us of our putting down the poor man and elevating the rich one. "But you have dishonored the poor man . . . But if you show partiality, you are committing sin and are convicted by the law as transgressors" (James 2:6,9).

We tend to feel a "sistership" for those who think as we do, dress as we do, live as we live, *but only for them.* We are in the danger of being Pharisees, unknowingly, by wanting to teach others just like us and then have them feel the same way we do about the same people.

We can no more pick our family in God than we can in the flesh. Christ died for all, and the acceptance of His blood and forgiveness gives us a blood relationship with God's family.

"How long will you love being simple?" God asks us. In time, may we maturely answer, "let me see things as they really are and learn to love as you do."

Help me to grow up.

> *In the bitter waves of woe*
> *Beaten and tossed about by the sullen winds*
> *That blow from the desolate shores of doubt,*
> *Where the anchor that faith has cast*

Are dragged in the gale,
I am quietly holding fast to the
Things that cannot fail.

— *Anonymous*

And that's maturity.

THOUGHT QUESTIONS

1. Why are we tempted to stay naive?
2. How can we maturely do better with our time?
3. Why is the choosing of our companions so important?

Chapter 7
TO BE PURE

"Blessed are the pure in heart for they shall see God" (Matthew 5:18). What a promise! If we are pure in heart, we shall see God face to face "and tell the story saved by grace." It is not normal or natural to be pure in heart. This wonderful characteristic is learned.

In climbing the Christian ladder described in 2 Peter 1:5-7, we start with faith. Faith is the foundation of Christianity. The first thing we add to our faith is virtue. Some versions say, "goodness," or "you must work hard to be good," or "goodness of life," I remember reading a commentary on this passage some time ago that defined virtue as, "Clean up your life." That defintion has always stuck in my mind.

Now that you have faith, clean up your life. Throw out the trash. Discard the things that make you stumble. It takes a long time to know all that makes you fall. We can in good conscience do a lot of things as a new Christian that we will not be able to justify as an older one. Many things look acceptable to our young eyes that are not pleasing in God's eyes.

At the conclusion of this list of qualities to add to your life, there is a little phrase that is very potent. It says, "For as long as you practice these things you will never stumble (2 Peter 1:10c).

Practice is the key to godly living. Study for knowledge; pray for wisdom; and practice what you are learning. You start out with the milk of the word – the part that is easily understood and digested, and you grow gradually until you can eat the meat. 'But solid food is for the mature, who because of practice have their senses trained to discern good and evil" (Hebrews 5:14).

We are constantly adding virtue, cleaning up our lives, practicing what God teaches us is good. His list is different from ours, but in time, as we become like Him, our list agrees. We become pure in His sight, and we

75

shall see Him *if* we remain that way.

Why is it so much worse to see a bad woman than a bad man? Why do dirty words or profanity seem so much harsher coming from her lips than his? Why do we hope for women to be ladies when they are not?

I've heard it said, "Man was made from dust and woman was made from his rib so she is twice refined." Or, "God said it was not good for man to be alone, but after He made woman He said, 'It is very good.'" Mankind expects more from women than men though we are expecting less from women as the days go by. (This is sad for womankind and for mankind.)

God gives us examples of both good and bad women. "This is the way of an adulterous woman: she eats and wipes her mouth, and says, 'I have done no wrong'" (Proverbs 30:20).

The woman of folly is boisterous,
She is naive, and knows nothing.
And she sits at the doorway of her house,
On a seat by the high places of the city,
Calling to those who pass by,
Who are making their paths straight:
"Whoever is naive, let him turn in here,"
And to him who lacks understanding she says,
"Stolen water is sweet;
And bread eaten in secret is pleasant."
But he does not know that the dead are there,
That her guests are in the depths of Sheol.

       — Proverbs 9:13-18

"Suddenly he follows her, as an ox goes to the slaughter, or as one in fetters to the discipline of a fool, until an arrow pierces through his liver; as a bird hastens to the snare, so he does not know that it will cost him his life" (Proverbs 7:22-23).

When we think of the woman who is pure in heart and whom we want to emulate, our thoughts go back to the worthy woman.

Her children rise up and bless her;
Her husband also, and he praises her saying:
"Many daughters have done nobly,
But you excel them all."
Give her the product of her hands,
And let her work praise her in the gates.

       — Proverbs 31:28,29,31

How do we become pure in heart? By becoming pure in thought. What we think, we are. What do we think about all day? *What we put in our minds comes out of our mouths.* Great thoughts make great people, and pygmy thoughts make pygmies.

"Finally, brethren, whatever is true, whatever is honorable, whatever is right, whatever is pure, whatever is lovely, whatever is of good repute, if there is any excellence and if anything worthy of praise, let your mind dwell on these things" (Philippians 4:8).

The Phillips translation says it this way, "If you believe in goodness and if you value the approval of God, fix your minds on whatever is true and honorable and just and pure and lovely and admirable. Put into *practice* what you have learned from me and what I passed on to you, both what you heard from me and what you saw in me, and the God of peace will be with you."

Note the word practice here. Put into practice what you have learned and what you are learning. Could we find the courage to stop the unlovely talking among the sisters who will not pass the above tests? Could we say something kind and honorable and gracious?

The Bible tells us to "set our affections on things that are above." Deliberately *set* or place your mind on things above. Don't let it get off the track. Satan will see to it that the constant temptation is there to think about the unlovelies in life and in the church, for they are many.

THE KEY TO BEAUTY

Women are especially mindful of their faces. We need to recognize that good thoughts make us beautiful. Lovely thoughts make us lovely, I've heard it said that we cannot help what we look like before we are forty, but we can help what we look like after that. That saying is emphasizing that our thoughts show in our face. Euripides said, "It's not beauty but fine qualitites, my girl, that keep a husband."

"Let your mind dwell on these things" (Philippians 4:8c). *Dwell* is the important word here. Is it honorable the thought I just had? If so, dwell on that thought. Is it a good report? If not, put it out. Is it an excellent thought and one of praise? Keep thinking about that. Exchange the bad thought for the excellent one. This is the power of positive thinking taught by the Original Teacher.

How simple the teaching and how hard to discipline our minds to the task! We must learn the art of self-defense. We must learn to love ourselves enough to protect our minds against the wiles of Satan. He bombards our minds with what is false, dishonorable, injust, impure, and ugly. These things are not worth thinking about and cannot be praised. That is his list, and *we must not be ignorant of his devices."*

God stresses to the women how to look physically: "Likewise, I want women to adorn themselves with proper clothing, modestly and discreetly, not with braided hair and gold or pearls or costly garments" (1 Timothy 2:9). The Phillips translation says this verse this way, "similarly, the women should be dressed neatly, their adornment being modesty and serious mindedness. It is not for them to have an elaborate hairstyle, jewelry of gold or pearls, or expensive clothes, but as becomes women who profess to believe in God, it is for them to show their faith by the way they live. A woman should live quietly and humbly."

Be neat; be modest; do not dress too expensively or wear outlandish hairdo's. We have seen pictures of women in other days who had their hair extended up for several feet with pearls and flowers and birds entwined in the concoction. (Surely they must have had to sleep in a chair!)

God says, "Show your faith by the way you live not by the way you dress."

Here again, we must not go to either extreme. We must not overdress or underdress. I have seen religions that order their women to wear long sleeves, tight collars, long dresses, no makeup, granny hairdo's, black shoes, and no jewelry. Yet, the worthy women dressed in purple with God's approval.

BY LOOKING AT HIM

Do you remember the parable Jesus told about the man who had been possessed with a demon, and it was cast out? (Matthew 12:44). His house remained empty, and in time seven more demons came back with the first one. The moral of the lesson was that after his life was cleansed, and he was forgiven, he did not busily add substance. He left his house empty, and in time an empty house fills up with emptiness. That is all the world has to offer. Add it all up, and its sum is nothingness.

The Christian is supposed to be able to give a reason for the hope that lies within him. To be able to give an answer means to know your Bible. *To know your Bible is to fill your mind with fullness.*

The seed is the word of God. The seed begins to grow night and day. We don't understand how it works and don't have to. That's God's business. As the seed grows, we begin to change — first the shoot, then the ear, and then the full grain in the ear.

God is busy changing us, and He uses the word to do it. The word is perfect, converting the soul. *Every answer is there,* and God's wisdom is given when we ask for it. So, what is the result? We are daily changing and becoming like Him, and *He is pure.*

Our thoughts become as His thoughts and our ways as His ways. As it says in 1 Corinthians 2:13-16 in the Phillips translation:

> It is these things that we talk about, not using the expressions of the human intellect but that which the Holy Spirit teaches us, ex-

plaining spiritual things to those who are spiritual. But the unspiritual man simply cannot accept the matters which the Spirit deals with – they just don't make sense to him, for after all, you must be spiritual to see spiritual things. The spiritual man, on the other hand, has an insight into the meaning of everything, though his insight may baffle the man of the world . . . This is because the former is sharing in God's wisdom and . . . incredible as it may sound, we who are spiritual have the very thoughts of Christ!

By filling our minds with His word we become like Him, and our old life cannot move back in.

SOME CHARACTERISTICS OF THE CHRIST-FILLED LIFE

Because we are in Him and He is growing in us, we can endure sufferings. "All that live godly in Christ Jesus will endure persecutions" (2 Timothy 3:12). God is always shaping us into better vessels for His use.

"We are always on the forge or the anvil; by trials God is shaping us for higher things" – Henry Ward Beecher.

Suffering is a part of the plan. Do we think that only Christ should suffer? "Must Jesus bear the cross alone and all the world go free? No, there's a cross for everyone and there's a cross for me."

In time, we can even love our enemies. God never tells us to do something He won't help us to do. I can learn to make a decision to love my enemy before he has made the decision of his next plan to hurt me. Only can this happen to a life that is filled with His word.

As we grow we will become fearless. God doesn't give us a fearful nature. "For God has not give us a spirit of cowardice, but a spirit of power and love and a sound mind" (2 Timothy 1:7). If God doesn't give us a cowardly spirit, then who does? Satan.

God tells women not to be fearful with their husbands – respectful, yes, but fearful, no. Many women are very fearful, but with God's instructions and His wisdom, they can overcome this nature. By doing so, they will also please their husbands. Most husbands want a worthy companion but not a groveling one.

A HOLY WOMAN

This boggles our minds! How can we ever dare to think that *we* might be holy? I heard a preacher define "holy" by using another spelling, "wholly." That makes it easier to aspire to. We want to be *wholly* committed to Him.

God taught in both the Old and New Testaments that He was going to make His children holy. "Because it is written, You shall be holy, for I am holy" (1 Peter 1:16). What a job He has on His mind to take us, sinful as we are, and make us – holy. Or pure in heart. *The word still has the power, the dynamite, to make us holy.* Incredible as it may sound, we who are in training are becoming holy, and pure!

THOUGHT QUESTIONS

1. How do we become pure in heart?
2. How is a woman truly beautiful?
3. What should we fill our minds and lives with?

Chapter 8
TO LOVE THEIR HOMES

God would not tell the older women to teach the younger women:

1. to be home-lovers (Phillips)
2. to be keepers at home (K.J.V.)
3. to be busy at home (N.I.V., N.E.B.)
4. to be domestic (R.S.V.)
5. how to work in their homes (J.B.)
6. to be good housewives (T.E.V.)

if there was not a natural desire to do the opposite.

There has probably not been a time in the history of man when women were so tempted to leave their homes and their children as in this present generation. It is the present fad:

1. to find "oneself"
2. to be thought ignorant and common if you *choose* to be *only* a housewife
3. to have "peasant" blood
4. to be accused even of being lazy if you stay at home

Whose doctrines are these?

There are women who want to stay home and are not permitted to. There are wives and mothers who must work to be able to survive. There are husbands who not only command that their wives work when it is not necessary but also covet their wives' income. Forty percent of family income is provided by wives now. The latest statistics say by the year of

2000, 75 percent of women will be working away from home. There are temporary emergencies where a wife has to work, and there are those who work because they are bored at home and assign their responsibilites to others.

WHAT DOES GOD SAY?

He says that the young women should be home with their children. Christians know this. We cannot expect the world to go against their nature, but we *can* expect the church to. The world lives in darkness, but Christians must be the light of the world.

Don't *Christian* young women get bored at home? Surely they often do. God did not say that the *exception* of the rule would be to those women who feel unchallenged at home and feel that they will go berserk if they have to change another diaper or mop another floor.

God looks at the end of the matter while we are overcome with the daily routine! He tries to show us that women are the hub of the family. Take the women out of the home, and there will be chaos. *In time there will be chaos.*

He does not write all the reasons for His commandments. He just says, "Stay home." Have you ever thought how large the Bible would have to be if God wrote out all the reasons for His rules? He gives us the positives, and time teaches us the negatives. Faith obeys, and our will rebels.

The heartbreaking truth of the matter is that when the children are grown or are in those difficult teenage years, the rut has already been furrowed. It takes *daily living together* to learn to know our children. We need to be the ones who hear their words and bind their wounds and give them quality and quantity time. *We need to be there.*

KEEPERS AT HOME

Many mothers are *at home,* but they are not a *keeper of the home.* The house and the children reflect our busyness or slothfulness. A mother propped up in front of the TV in her robe while the children are disassembling whatever is not a keeper of the home.

A Mama in bed while her small children play can be guilty of criminal conduct. Would she pay a babysitter to do what she does? Children can get away from the best of mothers and be seriously injured or killed. It happens every day. Not only is the child destroyed but *often the marriage is.* The "what ifs" torture both parents. "If only I'd" rings in their ears for the rest of their lives.

Many young mothers do not realize how quickly children can kill themselves! Children don't know enough not to drink poisonous things, not to play with scissors or knives, not to reach up and pull a pan of boiling liquid off the stove, not to play with matches, not to go into the street, not to turn on the hot water while in the tub, etc. (They are naturally drawn to water, and drownings occur so quickly and frequently.) They seem prone to destruction.

BABYSITTERS AND PLAYSCHOOLS

More and more we are hearing about child abuse in these conditions. Not only are children being physically abused but also sexually. Most sexual deviates are the result of adults starting them on that way of life. And most of these adults were relatives or close family friends! The older women should be teaching the younger that it can happen to their children, too. Children often do not tell their parents of these abuses. They have an instinctive shame.

One night we left our little boy with a teenage neighbor who had been begging to keep him. We left him asleep to just be gone for about two hours. When we came back, everything seemed normal, but our neighbor told us that the sitter had left the house after we did and only returned just before we came back. The house could have burned down in that time, or he could have awakened and cried and known that he was alone.

There are capable and dependable sitters and schools, but they cannot compete with the care of parents *who love their children*. There are times we need to be gone and to be away for relaxation, but do we need to be away forty hours a week?

THE MAN'S PUNISHMENT

After Adam sinned, God placed on him and mankind the making of the living for himself and his family as long as he lived. This was not placed on women. Her punishment was pain in childbirth. She is the weaker vessel, and God knows that *she does not have the strength to do his work and hers!*

I read the other day in a woman's magazine how little time the men work at home. It was infinitesimally small — something like 23 minutes a day. Man believes that the home is the women's responsibility. This article also said that the more the man helps at home, the more he resents having to.

So, the working woman puts in her forty hours away from home and then has it all to do when she gets home. How long can she last physically, socially, and spiritually? Who pays the price for her weariness? The whole family and even God in her lack of service. There again, if she could only see the end of the situation, if she could know how it is to live with broken health and nerves, would she do it? No.

God told her that she was the weaker vessel and that she should be protected and be lived with in an understanding way. But she *thought* she was stronger than God knew.

History tells us that years ago when our forefathers and foremother moved here, the women could not survive those terrible winters. Most of them died before their time. I have seen the burial grounds in New England of some of those couples. The man would be buried with several wives — wives who did not live long.

Now women are living seven to ten years longer then the men, but it will be interesting to see if those statistics remain constant with the increase of the women working two jobs. (Seventy percent of married women with children who work have more heart attacks than those at home.)

THE MARKET PLACE

God places women in the home. This is her arena, her palace. "Let our sons in their youth be as grownup plants, and our daughters as corner pillars fashioned as for a palace" (Psalm 144:12). Pillars in a palace is God's wish for young women and older women, too.

When she leaves the home to go into the market place, she is in the man's arena, the jungle. The sweat and the thistles become a part of her daily life, and it is sad to see her become a part of that carnal world. I read an article the other day teaching working women how to be executives. It taught her how to toughen up and secure and keep the best positions. The suggestions were given to help her overcome her femininity and to develop more masculine thinking.

She leaves her home as a protected Christian lady, and she goes out to hear the ribald conversations and suggestions. Many times she feels she has to bear the sexual overtures of her boss or fellow workers to keep her job. She is thrown with other women that she would not have been with at home, and she can quickly pick up their ways if she isn't careful. The things that shocked her at first no longer shock. In fact, she gets to where she can pretty well return what is thrown at her. To survive in the world, she becomes like the world.

A woman goes against her finer nature when she has to compete with the men in the world. She has to learn different ways, and those things she learns do not make for a better Christian home and a happier husband and children.

WE'RE PICKING UP THE MEN'S HABITS

Many women are now stopping by the bar for a drink before they go home just as the men have done for years. "Office wives" are becoming legion. The women tend to confide more to the man they work with than the man they live with. Women who are sent off to other cities get lonely and soon meet lonely men. "Everybody's doing it" will ever be a temptation – even to Christians.

It has been observed and proved that most men who make less than their wives cannot bear the competition. There is more wife beating and more profanity in homes where the wife is richer than her husband.

Women are more self-sufficient and are not trying to adjust to their husbands as they once did. It is much easier to leave their mates than to make a go of it. More and more women are leaving home. It used to be the man who walked out on his responsibilities but now many women do, too.

Women are often hiring people to take on their responsibilites. A working women made the statement the other day, "What I need is a wife." She wants to come home to find a clean house, supper cooking, and the children looked after. So, she hires it done instead of doing it herself.

She is expecting other mothers to bake the cookeis and attend the PTA and to babysit for her. "Will you pick up my children, take them to the doctor's office, check in on them at home, pick up a few needed groceries, etc., etc.?"

She counts on other Christian women to do her part in the work of the Lord:

"You'll have to bake the cake, or bring a roast or whatever; I'll just buy some rolls and butter."

"I can't be in on the work day – that's the only day I'm home, and I have to do all the things I left undone."

"My work keeps me from attending the Ladies' Day and lectureships and learning sessions."

So, our women do not have the time they once had for growing. Time is precious, and *there is so little of it.*

Many men feel justified in being an inactive part of the church because of their work. They feel that they have the right – even the necessity – of getting out and exercising, because they are so tied down with their jobs. Working women are following their example.

Listen and think upon this scripture: "And the one on whom seed was sown among the thorns, this is the man who hears the word, and the worry of the world, and the deceitfulness of riches choke the word, and it becomes unfruitful" (Matthew 13:22). Not unfaithful, but unfruitful.

TEACH THEM TO BE
HOME LOVERS – NOT HOME LIKERS

It takes a long time to learn to be a home lover unless your mother taught you to be one. The worthy woman is our example. She made beautiful tapestries. She had time to be gracious and to live well.

She carried her food from afar. This brings to mind that her table was spread with not only ample food but a charming variety. She went to the trouble of feeding her household with delicacies. She had fresh fruits, fresh fish and vegetables in season. She knew where and what to buy, and she had the time to do it.

Her meals were planned and not thrown together at the last moment. She put her good mind to the task of feeding her family well. God has given us a sound mind, and He hopes that we will learn to use it in our homes.

What are some practical ways we can learn to be a home lover? Magazines for women have lots of hints and helps and pictures and ideas. If you cannot afford to buy them, go to the library. Visit women with imagination and note stores who decorate beautifully. Swap ideas with other friends. This can inspire us to be more home conscious. Be imaginative. Let other women copy *you!*

When our husbands are pleased with our efforts, it encourages us to try harder. When we know that our merchandise is good, it gives us self-confidence and pleasure.

Garage sales have inexpensive little treasures that can be used to beautify our homes and our tables. It doesn't take a lot of money to produce a lovely home, *but it does take imagination and time.*

I remember a widow who moved to a little city where I lived. She had little or no furniture. She bought some unpainted chests and tables and second-hand furniture, and she painted it all red, white, and blue. It was absolutely striking! I used to bring people over to show them her house. She painted some chests white and then put red knobs on them and vice versa. She picked up cotton rag rugs in the right colors. She slip-covered the other furniture. She put the rest of us to shame with her originality. Anyone can spend money, but not everybody can make their place look beautiful and *not* spend much money. *That is an art.* Probably a learned one.

Hospitality is a command, and today that falls at the door of the women. Do we dare experiment with recipes? Do we pick up artificial flowers, old dishes, colored napkins, and beautiful records to play while we eat? Have we thought about putting a candle in a bottle with a candle ring of grapes, letting it drip down, a centerpiece for a spaghetti supper? Or paper flowers and Mexican ceramics for Mexican food? Or inexpensive Chinese figurines and little bowls for Chinese food?

I remember visiting some of my sweet Christian friends who have a lot more money than we do, and they had such beautiful homes. I noticed they had a lot of candles and grapes. I could not possibly compete with their lovely furniture, but I could afford some candles and grapes. (My husband says we have enough candles to heat the house for the winter.)

ENTERTAINMENT

What do you do after dinner? It is pleasant to just sit and visit. Some would rather do that. Others would enjoy games and we keep a lot of them on hand. Password, Dominoes (even double nines), silly card games like Spoons and Slap can be exciting and fun. We have found a game called the Ungame which is wonderful to play with families or new Christians or older ones. Now that we are getting older, it is more our speed. It has additional subjects to be discussed, and we have six different categories that we can play. All the trivia games can be fun – especially Bible Trivia.

If you are young and active, there is croquet, volleyball, and ping pong. They are great in getting to know each other. It is the being together that is important. (Making homemade ice cream is always fun.) And fattening.

These things take planning and energy. Someone has to be the pusher, and it probably won't be the woman who has worked all day or the women who have preschoolers. It takes a strong body to do all the planning, cooking and playing.

Many husbands will not be put out. But I have noticed that even though one drags his feet and feels too weary to cooperate, that in time he enjoys it. Just get the ball rolling and have the attitude that this is going to be great, and usually it will be contagious to the rest of the family.

I remember with nostalgia a place where we used to live. There were about six or eight families, all with young children. Someone would call and say, "Let's go to the lake." We had a regular menu of cut-up potatoes to fry, sliced tomatoes, fried Spam, ice tea, and a homemade cake from a mix. We would go out and fry the meat and potatoes and get all the food assembled while the men fished, and the children hurt themselves, and then we would eat. Oh, those were the days, my friends. Inexpensive wonderful fun! (Some of those children are now deacon's wives, or preachers or elders.)

A CLAIM OF GODLINESS

"But rather by means of good works as befits women making a claim to godliness" (2 Timothy 2:10).

How can we better make a claim for godliness – with the home as our headquarters or a job away from home? We are to be known for our good works, *but it takes times to do good works.* And energy.

It is a good work to be with our children, to keep our homes, and to love our husbands. These are all good works *ordained by God.*

We are not to leave our small children and homes to do good works. The time will come, anxious as we are to be out and doing, when we can more easily regulate Christian work outside our home. We will be able to service those in need and *not neglect* our priorities.

A dirty house and neglected children only cause the blasphemy of the *world* about the Christian wife. Instead of being a light, we may become an object of ridicule.

The church and the world know what our homes look like. God tells us to go and look and learn from the worthy women of Proverbs. He says, in effect, "Go and do likewise."

HOW GREAT THE TEMPTATION

How great is the temptation to be away, to dress up each morning and be where the action is! How easy it is to lay down my burden of child-raising and to pick up the lesser burden of working out! How wonderful that extra income so I can dress better and furnish the house better. How BORING to be at home! I would go crazy in a week! (I hear this.)

(Most career women have to learn how to adjust to home-living when they choose to give up their careers. Just as women who leave home for a career have to learn how to get both jobs done.)

Who is in this temptation business? "Fall down and worship me and I will give you kingdoms and riches" (Matthew 4:8-9). Satan never tells you about the end of the matter and what prices we pay for such homage. He knows better than that.

The alcoholic wishes he had never had that first drink; the smoker wishes she was not addicted. The worker away from the home is addicted, too. 'I've seen both worlds, and I'll take his" and "You can't stop me," they say.

You're right. The older woman can't stop you, but she has the responsibility to challenge you to try it God's way. She has the duty to tell you what God says to women, and then *the choice is yours*.

I gave these lessons in several lectureships and am getting responses from young women who say they have gone back home, and are glad. I imagine I am going to get several letters that say, "Butt out." I won't live long enough to hear some of the same sisters say, "I wish I had done it God's way."

We are all "too soon old and too late smart."

WHAT DOES THE HUSBAND SAY?

Many husbands do not question the wife about her decision to work. They go along with the tide. Some of their mothers worked and their grandmothers, and it will be more and more like that for the coming generations.

Many husbands, who have been raised in the Lord and whose mothers did not work, do not want their wives to work but give in for peace at home. Many see their homes gradually deteriorating and divorce is rampant in the church in this generation.

Sad to say that there are husbands who *want* their wives to work and

would be hard to live with if the wife refused. They have become accustomed to that second paycheck and its benefits. Many wives are unconsciously teaching their husbands to be selfish.

I have heard it said that the thing that women hate worse than anything else is the feeling of being used. I have heard husbands say, "I'll put you out to work." This may cause divorces, too. A woman may lose respect for her husband, and God says that the number one need of a man is respect from his wife.

Many young husbands and wives want to get ahead too quickly and not wait on the Lord. The Lord loves to give, and He plans to elevate our economy as we live and give. He promises that He will add all "these things" when we put his kingdom first (Matthew 6:33). But we want shortcuts. We want it NOW, and the woman working gives it to us now. Often, the men are blinded to the cost.

Many women are leaving their husbands because their jobs have become so productive that they do not choose to stay married. They can support themselves, and they choose to live without him. Surely he would not have wanted his marriage to have turned out this way! Surely he would not have chosen to lose his children and home!

USING OUR HOMES
FOR FINANCIAL BETTERMENT

The worthy woman did! She made girdles and sold them. She made them at home. The home can be a place to help the family out financially.

Godly women and men need to be training their daughters to be productive at home after they marry. Think about the occupations that can be done at home without the family being neglected. Babysitting, cooking, typing, tutoring, piano teaching, bookkeeping, hair care, etc. *Our sons should be taught to make a good living — an adequate living for his family.*

Look at the want ads and see the jobs that are advertised or people wanting someone to work at home. Handmade garments or crafts have taken America by storm, and that was what girdle-making was.

The working woman now seeks homemade goods, babysitters, dress makers, house cleaners, etc. She now can afford piano lessons, etc. She can afford what the home-keeper can supply.

THE EMERGENCIES

If we are in a temporary emergency, a financial disaster, the woman may have to help for a little while outside of the home. Hopefully, this will never be. Somehow we always made it — even when my husband was out of work. God saw us through.

If you *have* to work, do it part-time if possible. Work while your husband is home with the children, if possible. Leave your small children with a Christian. Or better yet, leave your children with your own Mother. (Though she probably didn't leave you.)

Make your decision that you will put your money to the emergency and, do it! Make your decision that you will be back home as soon as possible, and *be back home!* Realize that God loves you and is concerned, and trust Him more and your own strength less.

Note as you work how much more it costs to work and how little you really can help financially. You have to have more gas for the car, often the second car. You cook differently – more expensive quicker meals, more eating out. You have to have more clothes; you have to pay the babysitter, etc. Your income taxes go up because of the second check, and remember that you may become addicted – or your husband may become addicted for you to work. *The kids will never be addicted to your being gone.* Have you seen the TV commercial where the little girl begs her mother not to work, and the mother answers, "How can we buy your expensive designer jeans?" Or have you seen the insurance commercial that asks a grief-stricken husband and children, "How can you make it without her salary now that she is dead?"

HOW DO WE GET OUR HUSBANDS TO SEE?

How do we get them to see that we need to be home? If he is a Christian, we show him Titus 2:3-5. We show him that we are unhappy in neglecting him and the children. We point out that our physical strength is limited. We help him to appreciate our wanting to have a clear conscience.

Really, we could point out the same things to a non-Christian husband. We work at having a clean house, good meals, and a happy home and show him the advantages of this. We are less tired and more loving and hopefully he notes this as we stay home.

> DEAR MEG: I'm 36 and this is my second marriage. Pete's a wonderful man, terrific with my son and very helpful. We are in love.
>
> So why am I writing? I just started working full time so we can buy our dream house. My job in a hospital is hard, physically demanding and very tiring because I work overtime.
>
> There never seems to be enough time for us. We are rarely alone, and our love life has lost its sizzle. I'm too tired to make love the way we did before, so I just crash from exhaustion.
>
> I'm crabby because I'm bone tired. We seem to be at each other's throats most of the time.
>
> Any advice that you can offer would be appreciated. – Bad way, Baltimore, Md.

DEAR BAD: Fatigue can sabotage the best of relationships. Don't let it ruin yours.

In your eagerness to buy that house, you are jeopardizing your health, too.

Please cut out the overtime. It will save your sanity as well as your relationship.

Exhaustion is no excuse for crabbiness or missed love-making, especially when it is self-inflicted.

We need to pray for wisdom to learn to live within our means. Cut up the credit cards. Learn to budget. Learn to give to God, sacrificially, for He promises to turn around and give it back, pressed down and running over. "Give, and it will be given to you; good measure, pressed down, shaken together, running over, they will pour into your lap. For whatever measure you deal out to others, it will be dealt to you in return" (Luke 6:38).

THE GOLDEN YEARS AHEAD

How beautiful the second honeymoon! Though we will always miss the children we have, there is the compensation of grandchildren.

Surely, *now* we can work full-time! Why? To keep from being bored with all that time on our hands.

What does God say to this? He says, "This is the time for the most good work you have ever done!" You are "on call," if you strive for the qualifications of God's older women. You can be just as busy as you choose to be.

HOW DOES HE FEEL?

Many older Christian women do not allow themselves to see the yearning in their husbands' faces as they leave the home for work.

Many men realize that their time is limited on this earth, and they want her to be with them as their own time allows. There is no pressing need for *things* now. But there *is* a dire need for each other.

A HOME LOVER

So, when is the *convenient* time for the woman to leave her home? Never. Because "it takes a heap of living in a house to make it home" – Edgar A. Guest.

God appeals to us to be ever homesick for heaven. We are strangers and pilgrims here with temporary places of abode. He takes us from our "pleasant houses" to the home over there.

Proverbs 24:3-4 says it this way:

By wisdom a house is built,

And by understanding it is established;
And by knowledge the rooms are filled
With all precious and pleasant riches.

The Lord said, "In my Father's house are many dwelling places; if it were not so, I would have told you; for I go to prepare a place for you" (John 14:2).

The Lord says, "Come and see my home." When a woman loves her home, she, too, says, "Come, see my home, not my house, but my home."

Father, help us women to always want to do your will. May our lives be a blessing to your name, and may Jesus be glorified by our examples as mothers, wives and workers. Please help us to truly love our homes more and to make the right decision for them that would please you. Please be proud of us – your daughters."

In Christ's Name, Amen

THOUGHT QUESTIONS

1. What is a home-lover?

2. Why is the marketplace so attractive?

3. What do you do with a husband who pushes his wife to work away from home?

Chapter 9
TO BE KIND

The little foster boy prayed thus, "Lord, help the bad people to be good, and the good people to be nice."

Why, oh why, is it so hard for Christian people to be kind? Why do we have to *work* at compassion, gentleness, a pleasant disposition, a friendly touch, and mercy? Shouldn't those qualities be natural now? Can't our time be spent rather on the study of the law, the plumbing of the mind of Christ, and the chewing of the meat of the Word?

Reason agrees. But study tells us that by nature we are *children of wrath!*

> *And you were dead in your trespasses and sins, in which you formerly walked according to the course of this world, according to the prince of the power of the air, of the spirit that is now working in the sons of disobedience. Among them we too all formerly lived in the lusts of our flesh, indulging the desires of the flesh and of the mind, and were by nature children of wrath, even as the rest.*
>
> — Ephesians 2:1-3

It is natural to be "wrathy." It is natural to lose our tempers and be unkind. It is natural to say what we think in a certain tone and let the chips fall where they may. This spirit is still working in the disobedient, but we are not allowed the luxury of being unkind. We can't do what we please but what we must.

When you look back to a time you felt that you were justifiably right in blowing your cool and saying what you said, does it give you comfort now? Would you like to replay that scene with a different ending? I would.

"Temper"

When I have lost my temper, I have lost my reason, too.
I am never proud of anything which angrily I do,
When I have talked in anger, and my cheeks were flaming red
I have always uttered something I wish I had not said.
In anger I have never done a kindly deed, wise.
But many things for which I felt I should apologize.
In looking back across my life and all I have lost or made,
I do not recall one single time when my fury ever paid.

– Anonymous

We've all known people who were even tempered – always mad. Can a growing Christian be comfortable in continued sin? Of course not. Disobedience and unbelief are synonymous. What is the answer then? The answer is the hardest task in the world and that is dying to self. Becoming a new creature – crucifying the old person. *God never commands us to do something He won't help us do.*

This cannot be done without the help of the Godhead. Paul said, "I die daily" (1 Corinthians 15:31). It is a daily walk and a daily death. *Unless* we pick up the cross daily, we cannot be His disciple (Luke 9:23). It gets down to the nitty-gritty, this walk with Him.

It is interesting where God put this instruction to be kind. He put it after learning to be a home-lover and before submission to our husbands. There must be a connection. A kind woman's hospitable home often leads to the same future elder's hospitable home.

All Christians are taught to be kind. "Be ye kind one to another, tender hearted, forgiving each other just as God in Christ has also forgiven you" (Ephesians 4:32).

The world expects women – or used to expect women – to be soft spoken, easy to entreat, and nice. The world expects men to be aggressive, businesslike, feet on the ground, no nonsense attitude. God expects His women *and* men to be kind like Jesus was.

Jesus continually showed us how to walk the new life when he was here on earth. He was never on the defensive. He knew what was in the hearts of men, but He loved them anyway.

He taught us to be as gentle as a dove. Too often we are as harmful as the snake! Matthew 10:16 says, "Behold, I send you out as sheep in the midst of wolves; therefore be shrewd as serpents and innocent as doves."

Our attitude toward the lost is, "I'll save you if it kills you." We need to leave the unsaved friend as a friend with the door open for future conversations. The world and the church have about as many problems as they can handle. The Christians has the problems and the solutions. Hopefully, as the world sees your ordered peaceful life, they are drawn toward you. My husband, Russ, says, "Gentleness will prevent many miscarriages in the born-again process." The truth has the power to convert the soul, but it needs to be in the hands of the kind. "The servant of the Lord must not strive." or "The Lord's bond-servant must not be quarrelsome, but be kind to all, able to teach, patient when wronged, with gentleness correcting those who are in opposition, if perhaps God may grant them repentance leading to the knowledge of the truth" (2 Timothy 2:24-25).

We must let the word cut between the spirit and the soul, for it is *that* *sharp.* But the wielder of that sword must not cut but be gentle and kind.

JUDGMENTAL

Do you think Christians are harder on other Christians than they are on the world? I can see lots of heads nodding. We talk and sing about how great it is going to be when *we all get to heaven* for eternity. But strangely, we have to work and pray to get along with each other in the kingdom on earth.

We are all stumbling along this narrow road, and a friendly helping hand would be welcome. We are children; we are sheep; we are young; we are terminal; and we don't know how to go out and come in. We are in need of mercy and compassion.

> *Broad is the way that leads to death,*
> *And Thousands walk together there.*
> *But wisdom shows a narrower path,*
> *With here and there a traveler.*
>
> *– Anonymous*

God gives us the right to judge our brother's fruits but not his thoughts or motives. A good test to give ourselves when we find ourlves criticizing our brother or sister is, "Are you taking the position that this one is lost and going to hell if the world ended today?" Most of us would back up and not go that far. Then, if they are not lost and God approves of them, who are we to disapprove? Ouch!

> *"Surprise"*
>
> *I dreamed death came the other night and heaven's gate swung wide.*
> *With kindly grace an angel ushered me inside.*
> *And there to my astonishment stood folks I'd known on earth –*
> *Some I'd judged and labeled as unfit or little worth.*
> *Indignant words rose to my lips, but never were set free.*
> *For every face showed stunned surprise, no one expected me!*
>
> *– Anonymous*

Somewhere I read this quote: "Young preachers spend the first ten to fif-teen years preaching to the sinner, the next ten to the church, and the last part of his life concentrating on his own lack."

Kindness should come with age but does not always.

GETTING IN GOD'S WAY

Many women tend to help God out. The maternal and bossy spirit go hand in hand. We must be careful lest we become a meddler in other's business though we feel our motive is right. God may say, "Lady, don't try to help Me. You'll only confuse yourself and slow down My process." We see this spirit in Peter at the Transformation when he said, "Lord, let us build three tabernacles here." He tried to take over, but it was God's show.

None of us wants our faith questioned. Yet, if we only knew and be-lieved that God knows about the situation, is working on it, and will change it if it needs to be changed! If in "casting our cares on Him," we can let go and let God, it will spare us a lot of worry and unkindness.

God is not a hard task master, *but too often we are!* God gives justice and mercy. If we are not careful, we will ask justice for the brethren and mercy for ourselves.

I read a book the other day written by a lady psychologist, and she remarked that we need to remember that most of the world is only three years old. How much kinder we would all be if we treated each other as we would treat the toddlers or as we treat our pets. (Personally, I'll take any kindness that comes my way. I need it.)

THE MOST DIFFICULT KINDNESS

Hospitality is a hard saying and an almost forgotten art with the ma-jority of Christian women. It doesn't come easy. There are a few in each congregation who open their homes. *Very few.*

God's highest list for men to aspire to is the qualifications of the elders of the church. To be an elder he must have a hospitable nature. Now, a man can be just about as hospitable as his wife lets him be. (Who goes back the second time to a cold hostess?) But he has to learn along with his wife and children the price of hospitality.

It is like the art of learning to give. *It is giving.* It takes time before it is a pleasure. It used to be in the Old Testament times that the men were avid hosts. They felt the responsibility of entertaining and protecting their guests. Abraham fed the angels, and Sarah eavesdropped in the tent. (Eavesdropping is easier.)

Today, hospitality falls upon the women. It is her job to clean the house, buy and prepare the food, entertain the guests, and do the cleanup afterwards. Yet, God reminds him that she is the weaker vessel.

God says the elder must be *given* to hospitality. He must take the lead. And how it helps if he will! The most hospitable home I was ever in was one of an elder who took the lead. When we think back about visiting his home, we think of *his* graciousness, though she was too. He met us at the door. He seated us. He fixed the barbecue. He saw that our plates were kept full. He ate last. He kept the conversation going, and he made us feel like we were *extra special* to him. (I still think we were.)

I believe that more women would want to be more hospitable if the husband would take the lead. It is hard for the hostess to keep the conversation going when the men won't talk. She is afraid that she will be labeled empty-headed and a chatterbox if she continues to try to keep the conversational ball rolling alone.

THE SHARING OF OUR HOMES

Our homes are our castles, our hiding places, our bulwarks, our havens, and where we are *the most vulnerable.* Visitors see the cobwebs, the dust, the mice droppings, the mistakes and undones of our lives. I remember going to a friend's house too early one morning, unexpected. She peeked through the door with her hair in rollers and was still in her bathrobe. "Oh, it's you. *You* can come in." Which meant if it were anyone else, she would bolt the door. (A dubious compliment but one I understood.)

Guests see the tension of the home. They see the lack of cooperation between the husband and wife, if it is there. They see the discipline or lack of it with the children. They see the emphasis of the setting of the table and the quantity and quality of the food. *They see us!*

And yet, paradox that it is, they also see the love and humor and fun and quality of that home, if it is there. There is no way to learn to love each other more than to eat together! The early church spent a lot of time eating together from house to house.

God put one of the greatest heartbreaking sentences on the one who was withdrawn from when he said, "You can no longer eat together." That would not be a hard sentence today, for the disciplined brother would say, "I'm not going to miss what I've never had."

THE GUEST LIST

There are two kinds of hospitality. There is the "Gentile" list. It is asking someone who will ask you back. It is having your "buddies" in or your family. It can be "cliquey." *It is the same group all the time.* Even though the group may be Christians, they are still your closest friends.

We are allowed some Gentile time, but it is doubtful that it will be counted as good works. Everyone loves to be with his or her best friends and family. That's natural, but we have already discovered that "natural" is not the best way. For this sort of get-togethers, we can use either extreme — sterling silver, china, and flowers or potluck and paper plates. We are more tempted to "overdo" with this group.

With most rich people, the chief enjoyment of riches consist in the parade of riches, which in their eyes is never so complete as when they appear to possess those decisive marks of opulence which nobody can possess but themselves.

— *Adam Smith*

GOD'S LIST

The next list is not in demand. It definitely goes against nature, but it is the list that will be remembered by the Lord.

"Then they themselves also will answer, saying, 'Lord, when did we see you hungry, or thirsty, or a stranger, or naked, or sick, or in prison, and did not take care of You?' "Then He will answer them, saying, 'Truly I say to you, to the extent that you did not do it to one of the least of these, you did not do it to me.' "And these will go away into eternal punishment, but the righteous into eternal life" (Matthew 25:44-46).

The least of these is mentioned in an earlier verse: "And the King will answer and say to them, 'Truly I say to you, to the extent that you did it to one of these brothers of Mine, even the least of them, you did it to Me' " (Matthew 24:40).

We are to go out into the highways and the hedges and invite people to the feast of the Lord. And He also went on to say to the one who had invited him, "When you give a luncheon or a dinner, do not invite your friends or your brothers or your relatives or rich neighbors, lest they also invite you in return, and repayment come to you. But when you give a reception, invite the poor, the crippled, the lame, the blind, and you will be blessed, since they do not have the means to repay you; for you will be repaid at the resurrection of the righteous" (Luke 14:12-14).

You don't have to worry with this second list that your house will not pass inspection. Even tension should lessen. Quality will not have to be stressed in preparation or serving. *Quantity is always important.*

This reminds me of the little story that most of us have read in a bulletin. Two cold children were invited into a lady's house for hot cocoa. The little girl said, "You must be rich." "Why would you think that?" the hostess asked. "Because your saucers match your cups," replied the little girl.

And we are rich God blesses us so bountifully. "But they who seek the Lord shall not want of any good thing" (Psalm 34:10). He promises to supply our needs and to increase our seed for sowing. The oil and the flour still sustain our daily needs. "Rust is going to be our witness" against us. I am afraid. Ruth Renkel once said, "The best gift one can give a lonely person is an hour of your time." Someone thinks within herself, "But there will be breakage, even stealing of my goods, and the stress of dealing with undisciplined children." You'll survive. It is surprising how little of that there really is. Remember it is all going to burn some day anyhow.

TEACHINGS

"Be hospitable to one another, without complaint" (1 Peter 4:9). "To one another," have an open-house feeling in your heart, for when the need arises or just for fun. We have an example in Proverbs of a selfish man's hospitality: "Do not eat the bread of a selfish men, or desire his delicacies; for as he thinks within himself so he is. He says to you, "Eat and drink! But his heart is not with you. You will vomit up the morsel you have eaten, and waste your compliments" (Proverbs 23:6-8). It is uncomfortable to be the victim of forced hospitality.

"And into whatever city or village you enter, inquire who is worthy in it; and abide there until you go away. And as you enter the house, give it your greeting. And if the house is worthy, let your greeting of peace come upon it; but if it is not worthy, let your greeting of peace return to you. And whoever does not receive you, nor heed your words, as you go out of that house or that city, shake off the dust of your feet" (Matthew 10:11-14).

Would *our* house be chosen? Would *we* welcome in the stranger with no baggage? Would he stand outside our door and shake his feet so that God could see that he knew that he was not welcome during his stay?

"Let love be without hypocrisy. Abhor what is evil; cling to what is good. Be devoted to one another in brotherly love, give preference to one another in honor; not lagging behind in diligence, fervent in spirit, serving the Lord; rejoicing in hope, persevering in tribulation, devoted to prayer, contributing to the needs of the saints, *practicing hospitality*" (Romans 12:9-13).

"Practice hospitality." Practice makes perfect. There is a lot we can learn about sharing our homes and tables with practice. One of the hardest lessons I had to learn was to be moderate in my serving. If a large family came for a few days. I cooked a turkey and a ham and all the in betweens that go with those – cakes and cobblers, etc. I couldn't do less with a clear conscience. *I can now.* (Occasionally!) I learned with practice the price of what it does to me emotionally. It sets me in the frame of over-doing and frustration before the company ever arrives.

Maybe we get more influenced by the term "entertaining" than hospi-tality. I have been long on entertaining and short on hospitality. The elder who was so hospitable did not seek to entertain us. He just served us and loved us. Practice may teach us that.

Have people in because of the kindness of your heart, and be kind to them while they are there. And, leave a kind feeling between you as you part.

Practice and wisdom teach us that there should be a time limit on the invitation. Many times a Sunday afternoon lunch goes into a six hour afternoon stay and two meals served. We all need some rest on Sunday. We need to spell out in the invitation that the family retires about 3:00 for a nap. I have seen new Christians practicing hospitality and asking people in on Saturday night who were not Christians or were new ones. And I have seen those guests stay until the wee hours of the next day and the sleepy Christians appearing for worship while their guests slept on. Practice learns that Sunday starts on Saturday, and a good night's sleep is a part of drawing near to God.

You know He wouldn't have to teach us so much about this art if it were not a difficult assignment. There is very little — if any — teaching on being *available* for a dinner invitation. (That is one of those things that comes naturally!)

BE KIND TO YOURSELF

Serving comes hard. We would not want to be a burden to a willing Christian hostess! We would want her to make it easy on herself. Yet, we often make it hard on ourselves. We need to have an easier menu, time to rest that day, and a shared cleanup afterwards. I never mind helping to clean up, and we must realize that they don't either. In fact, some quality visiting is allowed when the two ladies get to talk and the men and children withdraw. If the men want to clean up, let them. The men will have some quality time together, too. And the kids will not only see the examples of hospitality, but also they will have warm and secure memories. (Some hostesses really prefer doing it all alone.)

Then, take it easy the next day, if possible. Rest, read, and relax. You deserve it! It will make you consciously or subconsciously not dread company as you used to. *God doesn't want it to be an ordeal.* He will help us and give us wisdom as we ask for it and as we practice the procedure.

Communicate to your husband and children how much you need them as you do what God wants you to do. Let them realize that service is being like God and that love should make us want to help the weaker vessel. There is a lot in pre-teaching before the company comes and in talking later about the result of the last company.

The worthy woman in Proverbs was wise and kind. "She opens her mouth in wisdom and the teaching of kindness is on her tongue" (Proverbs 31:26).

This also can lead to submission as the two work together to please the Lord. Remember that God made the list for the older women to teach the younger, and he put kindness between being a home-lover and submission. He said that the woman is to be a lover of her home, and the elder is to be a lover of hospitality. Her submission, though she is a home-lover, will kindly lead to sharing their home as he desires to do.

It is my conviction if we would restore this lost art and open our hearts and our homes to those who need us, that the church would again be the leading religious group of America! *Women are so important in God's plan of redemption.* He meant for them to have the time and inclination to be known for good works. There is no better work than this, for it leads not only to conversations but to a strengthening of the brotherhood – and an agape love for each guest.

"Choose you this day whom you will serve . . . but as for me and my house we will serve Jehovah." And tables. It's easier than foot washing! *Or maybe God counts it as foot washing!*

DON'T MAKE THE IN-LAWS OUTLAWS

Men are told to leave their parents and cleave to their wives. Women ususally cleave to their parents.

The children know their mother's parents best because Mother goes home as much as possible. Kindness teaches us that our husbands want to go home, too. And his parents yearn for their grandchildren as much as her parents.

Can we learn to be fair? Can we stifle our own selfishness? Will we conscientiously endeavor to do better from now on?

"When we are born into an earthly family, we're given the spirit of man; when we're born into the spiritual family, we're given the Spirit of God" – Anonymous.

One of the fruits of the Spirit is kindness. Goodness is another. Gentleness – another. "Against such things there is no law."

Remember your son will marry, too, someday and you,too, will be a mother-in-law!

FOLLOW AFTER PEACE

"Pursue peace with all men, and the sanctification without which no one will see the Lord" (Hebrews 12:14).

"Always be wanting peace" (J.B.).

"Aim at peace" (N.E.B.).

"Let it be your ambition to live at peace" (Phillips).

"Make every effort to live in peace" (N.I.V.).

The mood of the women usually permeates through the house and is "catching." There is going to be discord in the best of homes. How blessed is the home where the mother "follows after the things that make for peace" (Romans 14:19).

War belongs to Satan, but peace belongs to God. Someone has written:

"That's Life"

What seems to grow fairer to me as life goes by is the love and grace and tenderness of it, not it's wit and cleverness and grandeur of knowledge — grand as knowledge is — but just the laughter of children, and the friendship of friends, and the cozy talk by the fire, and the sight of flowers, and the sound of music.

— Anonymous

God has given to women this job: the pleasure of setting the stage, the home of comfort and sensual beauty, and the sound of peace.

How good He is to us women! How necessary godly women are in His plan for order and harmony! How blessed the homes of worthy women! Are *we* known as kind hospitable women?

THOUGHT QUESTIONS

1. Why are Christians harder on each other than they are on the world?
2. Why is hospitality a difficult kindness?
3. Name some ways we can "follow after the things that make for peace."

Chapter 10
TO BE SUBMISSIVE

God is so wise. Note His order in this instruction to the teaching of the young women. Teach them first to love their husbands, then to love their children, etc. At the end of the list, He says for them to learn to be sub-missive to those husbands.

God doesn't put this at the beginning of the instructions but at the end. And just before He gives this teaching, He puts in kindness.

Husbands, all husbands, yearn for kindness, peace, and a woman who will adapt to his lead. Do you remember the survey we quoted where men put compatibility at the head of their list of "wants"? In essence, a man's desire, "I want a woman I can get along with most of all."

THE MARKET PLACE
He spends most of his working time away from home. His thoughts are bought by his employer, also his energy and his youth. His body needs rest, and replenishing at the end of the day. His soul needs rest, too, and peace, love and understanding. He marries and takes a wife for life, "in sickness or in health, rich or poor, till death do us part." There is a contract made by two adults.

Though he leaves the market place for his home, the world still presses in on the family. The desire for luxuries are ever present. The strife of discord lurks, and the TV brings in its suggestions for what the world thinks it needs.

If we are not attuned to the word of God and if our eyes are not looking toward the only light there is, our reflective light may flicker and die.

BEING SUBJECT TO THEIR OWN HUSBANDS
In God's instructions to the older women on the list of what to teach the

younger women, He started the list with loving their husbands. Now, the list circles back to the relationship between the husbands and the wife. God stresses the importance of this tie, for the husband is the encircler. We must remember all the in between instructions, such as being sensible, loving the children, being kind, chaste, discreet, etc. But, the beginning thought is to love our husbands, and the ending thought is to adapt to them. To encourage their lead.

Let's consider some of the other versions and see if we can pick up any fresh thoughts on this verse:

"Being kind and obedient to their husbands" (L.B.).
"And be gentle and do as their husbands tell them" (J.B.).
"Who obey their husbands" (T.E.V.).
"Willing to adapt themselves to their husbands" (Phillips).
"Submissive to their husbands" (R.S.V.).
"Respecting the authority of their own husbands" (N.E.B.).

It used to be in the marriage ceremony the bride was asked to say that she would obey her husband. I don't think this is included in the vows anymore. It has become old-fashioned and archaic to feel that women are expected to be obedient any longer.

What does God say? He wants us to have a loving happy home. It is a credit to Him when we can show the world that Christianity produces happiness. He is spelling out to the younger women that the home will be happier for them if they are gentle and kind and obedient to their husbands. It takes faith to believe it, but it is so!

What would you give for peace? It's price is above rubies! There has to be a place "where the buck stops," a place for the final decision. God says the man is to take the lead, and the woman is to follow.

All men won't lead, and all women won't follow, but the ideal is for the man to diligently take the oversight of his household. The ideal is for the captain to sail his ship with order and discipline. The ideal is for the president of the company to know his workers and to superintend his plant and to make it a success. When failures come, the responsibility goes back to the head of the establishment, not the crew.

Many foolish women tear down their own houses. "A wise woman buildeth her own house but the foolish tears it down with her own hands" (Proverbs 14:1). We are in the generation that will go down historically as the time of the disintegration of the homes of America.

The mothers are gone; the children on drugs, and the husbands are in shock! What happened? Is there any way to turn the tide back? Can order be restored? In the world, probably not. In the church, we have the answers in the Word of God, but do we have the faith? Or inclination?

Is working out, working out? No. Aren't women to be their husbands helpers? Yes. What if a man cannot support his household without the help of his wife? Let's go back and look at the worthy woman one more time.

Did she help her husband financially? Yes. Did she leave the home to do it? No. She made girdles and sold them. (A lot is said about how much she sewed. Evidently, that was her talent.)

There are many talents that we can use at home that can be a lot of help financially to our husbands. We mothers need to see that our daughters develop ways of helping financially. Tutoring, piano lessons, typing, book-keeping, baking, sewing, craft making, and many other various talents can be honed and perfected and used if necessary. And yet the "hub" is home.

THE PRICE

Most Christian women admire a gentle, kind and obedient wife and wish that they were more like her. We can all write a list of names of women who seem to naturally have the sweetness and submissive spirit that is to be yearned for.

How we note the young people who are polite and pleasant and show the training of a good home! We want to raise that sort of young people. We want to have a loving relationship with our husbands and to raise marvelous children. Don't we?

This is why we need to take to heart this teaching in Titus, for it is the recipe for a happy home. It can be ours if we read, work and pray to that end.

I remember the story of a famous pianist who played at a concert. A fan rushed up and said, "I would give the world to be able to play like that!" The pianist answered, "No, you wouldn't because you wouldn't practice the hours a day that it takes."

The moral to that story is would we put to practice what we know to do in doing our part to produce the kind of home that hard work takes? And discipline? Part of that disipline is to be kind and submissive to our husbands. This, too, is against nature.

The man has to learn to lead, and we are the helpers even in that. He is going to make many wrong decisions, and we are going to have to discipline ourselves with God's help to forgive him. Just as we have to learn to be a wife and mother and learn to love, he has to learn to lead and to be a good husband and father.

HE TRUSTS IN HER

"The heart of her husband trusts in her, and he will have no lack of gain. She does him good and not evil all the days of her life" (Proverbs 31:11-12).

It takes time for him to trust in her. It takes time to be trustworthy. Our husbands have to know that we are on their side all of the time. We need to be their best friend. We want this home to live and prosper and to be a monument to God. We need to tell our husbands over and over these things. (This does not mean we uphold his error or sin.)

HE TRUSTED HER FINANCIALLY

Statistics say that most divorces happen now because of finances. A wealthy man was asked one time to what he contributed his success in finance. He said, "I wanted to see how much money I would need to make before my wife could spend it all."

But the worthy woman "considers a field and buys it; from her own earnings she plants a vineyard." (How many husbands today would allow a woman to buy land?)

This woman could be trusted to be wise. Wise in her selection of land, wise in her need of land, and wise in using her own money to plant the land.

Some husbands, probably most husbands, have to learn the cost of purple and lands and warm clothes and running a household well.

On the other hand, young couples just getting married want to start out with what the older couples have attained through a lifetime. They do not realize the different stages of financial lows and highs that hve been experienced in their parents' lives. The bride today wants sterling silver and crystal. (Her mother or grandmother rejoiced when the ten dollar rent could be paid.)

God wants us to have a comfortable living and our pleasant houses. But He wants us to have them *in time*. We short circuit His plans when we strive for "things" to the disregard of home and happiness. He will richly supply our needs in His good time. Over and over, He tells us what He wants us to have. He tells us that He can give so much better gifts than we can give to our own children. But, He knows in His wisdom that we will not appreciate what we have *if we have it too soon*.

One day I was in the grocery line with the checkbook and wrote a check for the groceries. A young lady turned around and asked me increduously, "Do you have the checkbook? My husband would never let me have the checkbook." We had to *learn* to share it. Hopefully they will learn, too.

Surely the lack of leadership, submission and knowledge of God's Word will lead to an unhappy and unfulfilled life. Older women are charged with the responsibility to help out the young women. Patience is hard for young people, and yet the best way is the way of waiting on the Lord and growing together, trusting and trustworthy.

WILLING TO ADAPT

"Willing to adapt themselves to their husbands" was what one of the versions used for the term "subjection." The ideal way is for the husband to lead and the wife to adapt. Daily. With most decisions, he should lead, and she should follow. This means time together to discuss and to talk things over. Quality time as well as quantity. It is a means of progress. Shall we rent or buy? Trade cars now? Where can we afford to go for a vacation? Shall we buy new shoes for one of the children this payday, or can the shoes make it until the next one? Each day has its problems and decisions to be made, and we advance by making a good decision *together*. (We even learn through the wrong decisions – the painful ones.)

Communication is the key!!! It is *always* the key. "Following after the things that make for peace" is another factor. Treating our husbands the way we would like to be treated is a giant plus. To have sympathy for his position of having to make the decisions. Forgiving him for the wrong choices is another.

TENDERHEARTED

Now we can see God's direction when he puts kindness before submission. Kindness leads to submission *not vice versa*. When I get cross-ways with my husband and am super critical, I find that *I* have to step back and work on kindness. Then it all falls in place again.

I work at remembering that we are all children – sheep – and terminal. None of us know how to go in and go out. If I were leading, I wouldn't know the answers. It would be the blind leading the blind. The man usually thinks more wisely than the woman does. More horse sense.

God tells Titus, "Let the older woman talk this way to the younger. They will take it better from her than from you." Women can agree together that we are not long on a lot of the right answers. Our emotions get in the way. (Why does the door to door salesman prefer talking to us? *Because we'll buy!*)

"Be gentle and do as their husbands tell them." If you were a man, wouldn't you dread "going to the mat" for every decision? Wouldn't you appreciate it if she could be easily won to your way of thinking?

He put within womankind the desire for peace. We are unhappy when our husbands are unhappy or displeased with us. This desire for peace is a gift from God to both of us – the husband and the wife.

THE EXCEPTION

Though we are to follow their lead, we are not to go across God's commands. *God is always to come first.* "We must obey God rather than man"

(Acts 5:29).

If Sapphira had not agreed with Ananias in lying about their giving, she would have saved her own soul and life and maybe his. But, they agreed together to sin (Acts 5). If Abigail had abided by Nabal's decision to ignore David and his army, she would have been a party to a massacre of innocent men. But she did what was right. Our moral strength can be an unbelievable encouragement to our husbands. We cannot compromise on sin. We cannot agree together to sin nor can we blindly follow error.

God told women in 1 Peter 3:6, "Thus Sarah obeyed Abraham calling him lord, and you have become her children if you do what is right without being frightened." Do what is right and do not be fearful of the consequences.

We have all heard true stories of women who became Christians and then were abused by their husbands. It doesn't always work, but it usually does. It is the only chance we have for them and for their souls.

God gives love and protection to the weaker vessel in the admonition to the Christian husband that He (God) will not hear his prayers if he does not treat his wife as he should (1 Peter 3:7).

SUMMARY

God never commands something that He won't help us do. We are blessed if we have had in our own raising the example of a gentle, loving woman who helped to keep peace and order in the home.

But God's forethought provides for those of us who did not have that precious example. We, too, can learn how to cooperate and become the helper that we want to be. Older women should be our examples and teachers.

Young women should bear in mind that they, too, will be called on for teaching younger women someday. We have all heard that old saying that "as goes the home, so goes the nation." Something is wrong when well over half of the nation has divorced.

Part of the cause of this is the lack of solid homes who have produced children who have lost their way. Husbands must lead, and wives must follow for the happiness of the home and the pleasing of God.

"Love is not measured by how many times you touch each other, but how many times you reach each other" – Anonymous.

Be good to yourself. Love your husband and adapt to him.

THOUGHT QUESTIONS

1. Is submission really necessary to the Christian home? Why?
2. How can a wife prove to her husband that she can be trusted with the checkbook?
3. Name some results that occur when the wife willingly adapts to her husband.

Chapter 11
SO GOD'S WORD
WILL NOT BE BLASPHEMED

There are only a few words left – one more teaching still untaught. It is a very potent disturbing phrase given in closing.

It proves these teachings are not just casual advice but warnings for the soul (as all God's teachings are).

Are these words said as a plea from God to His daughters or are they a straight look-in-the-eye from the Father? Or both? We see examples of God in both circumstances under the old law.

We see Him plead and beg Israel to come back to Him, to return to righteousness. "Why will you die, O Israel." Or "For I have no pleasure in the death of anyone who dies," declares the Lord God. "Therefore, repent and live" (Ezekiel 18:32).

We also hear Him say, "As I swore in my wrath, they shall not enter my rest" (Hebrews 4:3). And He let them wander in the wilderness for forty years, children of God, until they died. Only two righteous men of the original travelers made it to Caanan.

Maybe the words are so rightly written that they can move the love of the tender-hearted or get the attention of the stubborn. *He knows how to do that.* The first are moved by His love and the latter by His power.

WHAT ARE THESE WORDS?

That the word of God be not blasphemed (K.J.V.).
So no one will speak evil of the message of God (T.E.V.).
So that the Christian faith can't be spoken against (L.B.).
So that the message of God is not disgraced (J.B.).
A good advertisement for the Christian faith (Phillips).

111

So that an opponent may be put to shame, having nothing evil
to say of us (R.S.V.).
Thus the gospel will not be brought into disrepute (N.E.B.).

Many times as we read the past ten chapters, especially for the young
women, Satan tried to jar the reception. He is a static causer. He tempts us
at our weakest points. Remember how many years experience he has had!
But, thank God, God is greater and much more powerful than Satan.
"Because greater is He who is in you than he who is in the world"
(1 John 4:4).
Satan's greatest tool is deceit. He fools us. He lies to us – *and we believe
him!* He is the father of every lie. He is after our *soul.*
Will we allow ourselves to believe that through our stubborness or
naivete we can be guilty of causing God Himself to be dishonored? Do we
believe that is even possible? Satan says it isn't.
Does the Father get *that* involved in our lives? Does He care if my husband is unloved or my children neglected? Does it really concern Him if
I am not a home-lover? Does He note my indiscretions, unkindnesses, or
lack of hospitality? Do I insult Him when I insult my husband? (That hurt!)
Does He care when I tear down my own house with my own hands and sit
and cry in the rubble?
But a much more important question is the one God is asking us – "do
you care when your actions hurt me?" And each of us will have to answer
that question individually.
God pronounces a woe to those who have evil and good all mixed up in
their thinking: "Woe to those who call evil good, and good evil; who
substitute darkness for light and light for darkness; who substitute bitter
for sweet, and sweet for bitter! Woe to those who are wise in their own
eyes, and clever in their own sight!" (Isaiah 5:20-21).
It is hard for women today to believe that the world is wrong and God is
right. We can't help being influenced by the conduct of others! Some
answer thus: "How can we live with being the only woman in the block
that stays home and is 'just' a housewife? This teaching is 2,000 years old!
I don't have the courage or inclination to swallow it." Yet His words echo
in our hearts, "I have plans for you, plans for your welfare and not for calamity to give you a future and a hope" (Jeremiah 29:10-11).
The real problem is getting our "want to's" straight. This is a *hard* decision.
But where does it say that being a Christian is easy? A cross is never easy
to carry or drag. But God tells us that the reward at the end of the way is
worth it all! I believe that. Don't you?
Pray about it. God's ears are open to His daughters. How quickly He
hears our petitions. Do you remember when good King Hezekiah was told
to get his house in order for he was going to die? Isaiah, the prophet, had

brought this bad news. Hezekiah wept and reminded God of his own good life and service. He begged to live. He cried. Note how quickly his prayer was granted.

"And it came about *before Isaiah had gone out of the middle court,* that the word of the Lord came to him saying, "Return and say to Hezekiah the leader of my people, 'Thus says the Lord, the God of your father David," I have heard your prayer, I have seen your tears; behold I will heal you. On the third day you shall go up to the house of the Lord, and I will add fifteen years to your life . . ." (2 Kings 20:4-6). "It will also come to pass that before they call, I will answer; and while they are still speaking, I will hear" (Isaiah 65:24).

That is how anxious He is to help us. But we often *have not* because we *ask not.* God hears the prayers of the righteous, but He turns away His ears when we won't listen to Him.

"For the eyes of the Lord are upon the righteous, and His ears attend to their prayer. But the face of the Lord is against those who do evil" (1 Peter 3:12). (What does God call evil? Disobedience of His word.) "He who turns his ear from listening to the law, even his prayer is an abomination" (Proverbs 28:9).

It is a two-way street, and because we care for Him, we will listen and revise our life. Come to think of it — isn't that what we are supposed to do daily?

We must remember it is His love for us that causes Him to give out the warnings and instructions. Will we take Him at His word or will we endanger His good name? The choice is ever ours. That's fair, isn't it?

God's plans for our welfare are always conditional. Be ever conscious of the "ifs" in the word.

In this key verse of Jeremiah He tells of His marvelous plans that He has worked out for each of us and then He gives the "ifs."

"Then you will call — come — pray, you will seek and find me when you search for me with all your heart." That's work, probably a lot of suffering, too.

"Lord, Are You Serious?"
Lord, do I really have to do everything you say?
Don't I get to do some things my very own way?
Isn't your book just full of suggested things to do?
Hints full of wisdom, proposals, often true?
Or are your words still "wonderful words of life"?
Could they really have the power to quench my pride and strife?

Surely in all this time they've lost some of their power
Can no longer give the strength to each waking hour.
But a solemn thought keeps probing as it ever comes my way.
"The words I've said will judge you when we meet on Judgment Day!"

— Lea Fowler

THOUGHT QUESTIONS

1. Why is deceit such a powerful weapon for Satan?

2. Are God's words commandments or just good advice?

3. What does the word blasphemy mean?

Chapter 12
THE BOTTOM LINE
or
DO I LOVE HIS WORDS?

Teach me to love every word that falls out of the mouth of God. Jesus was called "The Word." You can stake your very life on what He says. Many martyrs have. "And I saw the souls of those who had been beheaded because of the testimony of Jesus and because of the word of God" (Revelation 20:4b). Their torturers said, "Just deny Him and you will be spared."

When Solomon finished the inspired book of Ecclesiastes, he summed up his teachings by saying, "The conclusion when all has been heard is: fear God and keep His commandments because this applies to every person" (Ecclesiastes 12:13). The King James version says it this way, "fear God and keep His commandments for this is the whole *duty* of man." The word "duty" has been suppplied by the translators. I think it is more effective to quote the verse without the added word – duty. "Fear God and keep His commandments for this is the whole of man." *This is the bottom line!*

But, will we keep His commandments if we don't know what they are? Will we keep them if we do not continually refresh our memory of what is required of us? Can we ever be familar enough with the sixty-six books to rest confidently in our knowledge and memory? Who claims to be a scholar and not a student?

STUDY FOR GOD'S APPROVAL

Study – dig – understand. Be able to have God's approval for your expertise in handling the word of God.

"Be diligent to present yourself approved to God as a workman who does

115

not need to be ashamed, handling accurately the word of truth" (2 Timothy 2:15).

Use your Bible as a textbook. Don't be afraid that the book will be desecrated because you mark in it. Underline; make notes; use the references. Keep a good concordance handy. (The concordance in the back of your Bible is insufficient.)

Make your own references by inserting a scripture by the one you're reading. As you study, read the references, especially on a difficult verse.

Use many translations as commentaries. Always be mindful that any commentary or paraphrased version may be incorrect. But, don't be paranoid about checking out the words of scholars. A Greek lexicon is a handy tool. Don't be afraid of it. Make it a friend, a helper.

"But sanctify Christ as Lord in your hearts, always being ready to make a defense to every one who asked you to give an account for the hope that is in you, yet with gentleness and reverence" (1 Peter 3:15).

Learn the answers. You can. God will help you. Learn to rightly divide the word of truth. Who is speaking? Who is being addressed? What dispensation are they under? What is the context? The Old Testament and the first four books of the New Testament were written to people under the old law. The new law started after the death of Christ. The New Testament, the will left by Christ for His inheritors or heirs, went into effect after the death of the testator – Christ.

"For where a covenant is, there must of necessity be the death of the one who made it. For a covenant is valid only when men are dead, for it is never in force while the one who made it lives" (Hebrews 9:16,17).

THE LOVE OF THE LAW

We will never be Bible students until we love the law! We will never love the law until we diligently open the book. It is a treasure map with a pot of gold at the end of the rainbow. It is filled with goodly pearls that are found only by the seeker. The more you read, the more you understand. The deeper you go, the deeper there is still yet to plumb. It is informative, interesting, thrilling, scary, and as powerful as dynamite.

"For I am not ashamed of the gospel, for it is the power of God for salvation to everyone who believes, to the Jew first and also to the Greek" (Romans 1:16). The word "power" comes from the Greek word "dynamos" from which we get the English word "dynamite".

What else can cut between the soul and the spirit of man? We have difficulty even understanding that there is a difference between the soul and the spirit – let alone cutting between them.

"For the word of God is living and active and sharper than any two-edged sword, and piercing as far as the division of soul and spirit, of both joints and marrow, and able to judge the thoughts and intentions of men's hearts" (Hebrews 4:12).

Other versions:

"It cuts all the way through, to where the soul and spirit, to where the joints and marrow come together. It judges the desires and thought of men's hearts" (T.E.V.).

"It penetrates even to dividing the soul and spirit" (N.I.V.).

David, a man after God's own heart, loved the law he was under. Read carefully the 119th Psalm. Almost every verse is telling us how important it is to know the scriptures. It reminds us of the proper attitude that we should have as we read. It tells us of the rewards and punishments of the students and lawbreakers.

"If thy law had not been my delight, then I would have perished in my affliction. I will never forget thy precepts, for by them thou hast revived me" (Psalm 119:92,93).

"Oh, how I love thy law! It is my meditation all the day" (Psalm 119:97).

(I would suggest to ladies who use this book for their class study that they carefully and prayerfully use this whole psalm for further class time. There are twenty two sections to keep you busy. You'll love it and be richly blessed!)

MEDITATION

"But no one says, 'Where is God, my Maker, who gives songs in the night, who teaches us more than the beasts of the earth, and makes us wiser than the birds of the heaven?' " (Job 35:10-11).

Do you ever lie in bed and count your blessings? Do you wake up in the middle of the night and "sing songs of thanksgiving"? Do you sit in your comfortable chair or by the ocean or in front of a fire and let your heart meditate on God's ways and words? Do we truly appreciate how good He is to us, especially as we compare our lot with Africa and such like?

"Is anyone among you suffering? Let him pray. Is anyone cheerful? Let him sing praises" (James 5:13). In both instances there is an interaction between us and God.

In the book of Psalms, you will often see the word "Selah." That word means — stop and think about what you just read. Underline that thought! Meditate on it. Don't just read it — think about it.

Meditating time has to be taken. One could almost say "stolen." We are too busy! Too busy to read, to think, to pause, to take it into our hearts. We, too, trade our time for a bowl of pottage.

Waste is usually waste. Waiting on the Lord does not appeal to us. Don't you think our daily "closet" prayer (Matthew 6:6) means to spend time with God, talking to Him and thinking about His will for the rest of our lives? Meditating time.

EAT THE WORD

Jesus taught one of His most misunderstood lessons in John 6:48-69. In fact, it was so potent that many of His disciples left Him that day.

He taught them that He was the Bread of Life. He said that they could live forever if they ate this Bread. He even said that whoever ate His flesh and drank His blood abided in Him.

When the hearers began stumbling over this difficult teaching, He gave them their needed answers.

"It is the Spirit who gives life, the flesh profits nothing, the *words* that I have spoken to you are spirit and life" (John 6:63).

He was trying to teach them that His words are like bread. Eat them; devour them; digest them. You will never be spiritually hungry again. "My words are like eating a feast." But, this did not satisfy the many who left Him that day. Their thoughts were literal, carnal, but His teachings were spiritual soul food.

What was He saying to them that day that applies to us? In essence it was this, "Eat me; fill your minds and hearts with my words. Keep eating and drinking so you will be prepared for every good work and fortified for every foe. If you will do this, you will never starve spiritually. You will never die for lack of sustenance, for my words will sustain you."

We will never leave Him as those disciples did, *if* we are full of Him.

EZEKIEL'S ADVICE

"Now you, son of man, listen to what I am speaking to you; do not be rebellious like that rebellious house. Open your mouth and eat what I am giving you" (Ezekiel 2:8).

In Ezekiel 3:1-7 the Lord says:

> Son of man, eat what you find; eat this scroll, and go, speak to the house of Israel." So I opened my mouth, and He fed me this scroll. And He said to me, " Son of man, feed your stomach and fill your body with this scroll which I am giving you." Then I ate it, and it was sweet as honey in my mouth . . . I have sent you to them, who should listen to you; yet the house of Israel will not be willing to listen to you since they are not willing to listen to me.

God was teaching Ezekiel, His prophet, to eat His words, fill himself with God's truth, and then teach out of an abundant storehouse of knowledge. Yet He warned that the audience would not accept the teaching.

It is necessary for the teacher to be full of the word of God so that he can survive the rebellion of the hearers.

We should honestly ask of ourselves: Are we the student who constantly fills ourselves with the word or do we, too, walk away?

THE ANSWER BOOK

When I was a child, we occasionally had books in school that included the answers to questions asked or problems to be solved. These answers were in the back of the book.

God gives us a detailed answer book. He entreats us, begs us, to look to Him for a happy and abundant life. He wants us to have wisdom, to know how to direct our daily lives, to have a good marriage, faithful children, a loving husband, peace of mind, and finally how to get home to Him.

Often we want a quick answer with little study. We even want to copy another's paper. We want to pass the test and have all the blessings with as little involvement as possible. And that's impossible. We want to look in the back of the book.

We don't want to eat it or it to eat us. We gain a little "head knowledge" but not a lot of "heart knowledge." As I heard someone say, "We want to live like the rich man and die like Lazarus."

THE GIVER

God is Love, and God is the greatest of givers. He stands and knocks at the door of our hearts asking to come in and sup with us. He even provides the feast, literally and figuratively. *But He never force feeds.* Rather, His plea is, "Come, now and let us reason together" (Isaiah 1:18). The next verse says, "If you consent and obey, you will eat of the best of the land." Consent to what? Obey what? Sitting and reasoning with God.

One of the saddest verses in all the Bible to me is found in Ezekiel 33:11b. "Turn back, turn back from your evil ways! Why then will you die, O house of Israel?"

The church is the house of Israel now. We have our answer book in our hands. *What can be done to make us love it, study it, and meditate upon it?* Who can persuade us to take the gift of His word into our hearts?

SUMMARY

God, through Titus, instructs the older women to help the younger women. Hopefully the younger women will welcome the reasoning together of the two. Hopefully the younger will reach for the outstretched hand of the older.

"Door to Door Mama"

God sent me to you; will you let me come in?
I'm a "door to door" Mama, on needles and pins.
I don't want to pressure, just help with your load.

119

It's God's way of service; I'll not be a goad
Or a scolder or a cause of distress —
But rather a friend who understands the mess with which
Satan entraps us by his desire for our soul.
We want heaven, but that's not his goal.
Together let's reason and read from God's word and
Learn all the lessons yet to be heard.
We'll pray for endurance and take a long look at the
Wealth of the answers found in the Book.

— Lea Fowler

He gives us a list of things to talk about and to work on. And He closes the list with the thought that these things *must* be taught and practiced. If they are not practiced but are disregarded, then God's Word would be blasphemed.

This final chapter was written to emphasize that if we learn to really love His word, we will not only be free from blasphemy, but we will sail our ships to a safe harbor.

When all is said and done, we still have to ask ourselves: *How much do I really want to please God?* Am I pleasing Him now with the way my home is? Am I ready for every good work? Are my children and husband happy? Is Christ proud of me? Do I love the word of God and do I share it with others?

My sisters, my daughters, may I close with this admonition: "Pay close attention to yourself and to your teachings; persevere in these things; for as you do this you will insure salvation both for yourself and for those who hear you" (1 Timothy 4:16).

You will help to save your house. That's all Noah saved.

THOUGHT QUESTIONS

1. How do we get closer to the word?
2. What can cut between the soul and spirit of man?
3. How can we save our homes?

Chapter 13
TYING UP SOME LOOSE ENDS

The ladies magazines and many psychologists constantly tell us that the women who work away from home all day, all week, have a happier marriage than the woman who stays home. Is that so? Some agree, some disagree.

Just for fun let us assume that this is a true statement. Why could this be true?

Self-esteem, probably. Dressing up, having your own money, the leveling up of family responsibilities. (Which means that he *has* to help with the house – work and the kids.) More freedom from druggery. More equality.

The husband looks at the wife with new respect. "She's come a long way, baby." He fears for the first time her power. She doesn't have to be under his authority. She is around attractive men all day. There is not the respect that there used to be in her eyes or manner.

He has more to lose by losing her than she does by losing him. If she leaves she takes the nest and the children, if she wants them. They both would probably marry again and the children will experience the tug-of-war that results.

So, the man who was once assertive now tiptoes through the marriage. And the writers and psychologists conclude that this is indeed a happier marriage than the "traditional" one of old. Because of tip-toes.

But the scores are not in yet. There has not been enough time to evaluate the life style. Unfavorable results are beginning to infiltrate the media. Somebodies, somewhere, are beginning to add up the negatives. Many women are going back home, even successful business women, to have babies and give up their lucrative salaries.

I was reading a newspaper article the other day that said it is hard now for men to find mates. Women are choosing to wait for marriage and families. She is honing her skills and rising rapidly to the top of her profession. But often when she gets to the top she finds that she has not reached happiness and fulfillment. It is human to want it all.

This may not be all bad for the older single woman. Usually the older you are the wiser. Surely, there would be more careful choices in seeking a mate. There will be the advantage of starting out the married life with a more comfortable bank account. Many necessities and luxuries are bought and paid for.

When the decision is made to have a child, the child will be loved and taken care of. I remember seeing a program on TV where several famous older men were talking about how much better fathers they were to their "second" family. They remarked how they had neglected their older children and how they now delight in the younger ones. (Of course, most of these men were talking of their second marriage and the children of that marriage. I have often wondered how the "first" children felt as they see the adoration given their half-sisters and brothers.)

THE CHRISTIAN WOMAN'S SECURITY

The woman who stays home with her husband or her children cannot help but wonder if she is making the right decision. It seems "they" are happier, more prosperous, and that "their" home is more peaceful.

But God knows the end of the lives we are living. His values do not change with the years and the times. The same book works with the primitive man and the astronaut. (Many of the astronauts' homes have split up.)

God is aware of the physical limitations of women. He tries to shelter and protect them in just the way that He wishes the husband would do.

It is easy to gradually get on the merry-go-round and to think that life is better when it is noisier, faster, and the music is playing. But maturity teaches us that while we are hiding, the things we are leaving undone are growing and festering. Pay day eventually comes to all of us.

When we have carefully obeyed God's plan for women and our marriage falls apart and we are "put away" there is the constant comfort of obedience to God. Sad to say, this does happen occasionally.

If our children stray away from the Lord after we have taught them and trained them and were always there for them, we find the burden of their disobedience lessened. We find the strength to live with that heart-break. For we are mindful that God makes our children creatures of choice – not robots. (And some do fall away.)

But how do we handle losing our husbands or our children when we wouldn't listen to God's plans for us? How many times a day do those heart-breaking thoughts crowd in on us?

God really wants the best for us — happiness, security, loving husbands, and children, and heaven ahead. If we pursue happiness and self-worth we will usually be chasing after the wind. However, if we get a straight course to perfection and good works, we find that happiness is a by-product of obedience to His blue-print.

SELF-ESTEEM

As we think of the worthy woman we realize that she must have had loads of self-esteem though she was too busy to seek it. She was an overwhelming success in whatever she put her hand to. "A gracious woman attains honor" and honor was hers. Her good works praised her in the gates and ours can too.

Many women may someday well resent the brain—washing of her social sisters. "The truth is that all sound minds at the bottom are rational. Every man's self respect is appealed to when his reason is addressed; and every man, however much he may for the moment be pleased with the tickling of his fancy, will resent it in the end with revulsion of feeling, as if he has been imposed upon" — Bresee. Women are being imposed upon by non-Christian women. Remember that temptation is just that. It is something that goes against what is right — something we would rather do than what should be done.

There are women who feel that being a woman is a put-down. But it isn't! Being a woman is a blessing and an honor. God's woman is to be treated with honor. She doesn't have to triumph in a man's world. She is an equal heir in God's sight. "One of the best of women's rights is a right of exemption from men's duties."

The home is a proving ground for the future. The important decisions are made there — not in the market place. Day to day living and suffering and growing go on where we live. Every day's evil is preparing us for the things that war against our soul. It is using our time constructively.

MORE TIME-CONSCIOUS

How much time do we have left? When is the trumpet going to blow? God tells us to "redeem the time" — or buy it up. Many reason within themselves — "when we get this house paid for, then, we will begin to live." Or, "when the kids get in school or out of school — then things will be different — more orderly."

I remember asking a dear friend of mine why older people did not start living closer to God because they had to know that they were getting close to death. She answered wisely, "We die like we live."

Too many of us intend to try it God's way some day but not now. We put a distant goal in our minds when we will change and become more godly. But time cannot be counted on.

In fact, "Handling the stress of life is like handling a bank account. The Creator has deposited a certain amount of "adaptation energy" within us at birth, enough to last a life time. If we withdraw from that account excessively, we may one day discover that the account which cannot be replenished, is overdrawn" – John Haven.

We may be close to over – drawing by too many irons in the fire. Even a strong marine can break with battle fatigue. We think we will always be just as healthy as we are now, but we won't. What if we finally come to our senses and our bodies will no longer obey our commands? Or our minds? God knows all this and hopes to be permitted to pilot our ship to the shore.

Some one has wisely pointed out to us a profound truth. May we close this book with these thoughts?

> *I counted dollars while God counted crosses.*
> *I counted gains while He counted losses.*
> *I counted my wealth by the things gained in store,*
> *But He valued me by the scars I bore.*
> *I counted the honors and sought for ease.*
> *He wept while He counted the hours on my knees,*
> *And I never knew until one day by a grave*
> *How vain are these things that we spend a life to save.*
>
> – *Anonymous*

THOUGHT QUESTIONS

1. Have you read statements in prominent magazines that marriages are happier if the wife works away from home?

2. Have you heard lately of some movements of the tide turning and many women coming back home?

3. How can we build a good self-esteem at home?

SUGGESTIONS FOR FURTHER CLASS STUDY

1. Break the longer chapters into two or three parts.
2. Teach Psalm 119 by the sections found in the New American Standard, twenty-two divisions.
3. Read excerpts from the suggested books noted.

ON MARRIAGE

Understanding the Male Temperament or What Every Man would Like to Tell His Wife About Himself, But Won't	Tim La Haye
To Understand Each Other	Dr. Paul Tournie
Love Must Be Tough	Dr. James Dobso
The Road Less Traveled	Dr. Scott Peck

ON CHILD RAISING

How To Really Love Your Child	Dr. Ross Campt
How To Really Love Your Teenager	Dr. Ross Campt

(It is good for Christian women to build up a good library for her own u and for helping others. Most of these you can buy in paperbacks.)

MY PLANS FOR YOU

Lea Fowler

For I know the plans that I have for you,

Plans for your wel-fare and not for ca- lam- i- ty

—. To give to you a fu-—ture and a hope,

Then you will call Me and come and pray to Me.

Chorus

And I will lis-ten to you and you will seek Me and

find On- ly when you search for Me with all your heart —.

The chorus can be sung at the same time as the verse.

1. Teach the chorus first—Repeat.

2. Teach the verse next.

3. Combine them by singing the verse together. Then as one group sings the chorus, let the other group start the verse again. Then both groups can sing the chorus together at the end.